THE FAMILY GOD USES

Tom & Kim Blackaby

LifeWay Press®
Nashville, Tennessee

Published by LifeWay Press®
© 2009 Tom and Kim Blackaby

ISBN 9781415867099
Item 005189546

Dewey decimal classification: 220.07
Subject headings: BIBLE—STUDY \ GOD

This book is the resource for the course CG-1472
in the subject area Personal Life in the Christian Growth Study Plan.

To order additional copies of this resource: write to LifeWay Church Resources Customer Service; One LifeWay Plaza; Nashville, TN 37234-0113; fax (615) 251-5933; phone toll free (800) 458-2772; order online at *www.lifeway.com*; e-mail *orderentry@lifeway.com*; or visit the LifeWay Christian Store serving you.

Printed in the United States of America

Leadership and Adult Publishing
LifeWay Church Resources
One LifeWay Plaza
Nashville, TN 37234-0175

DEDICATION

To our children **Erin**, **Matthew**, and **Conor**—

You have been a continual source of joy, blessing, fun, and wonder.

You have challenged us to be better parents and better people.

You have taught us more about ourselves and more about our God.

We are forever grateful for the gift of you.

ACKNOWLEDGEMENTS

PRODUCTION TEAM

Kris Dolberry, Editorial Project Leader

Joyce McGregor, Content Editor

Darin Clark, Creative Direction

Denise Wells, Graphic Designer

Kailey Black, Production Editor

SPECIAL THANKS TO:

Micah Kandros, Cover Photography and Design

Amber Light Photography (Maple Ridge, British Columbia, Canada), Blackaby Family Portrait

Matt Evans for his contributions to this project.

Also special thanks to the Weimer family for "modeling" their hands for the book's cover. Here is their story of becoming a family God uses.

"My life is not my own. My life is not my own. My life is not my own. Since 2007 those six small words have become our family's mantra and have guided our steps as we devote our earthly lives to being a family that God uses. In early 2007, after having three biological kids, God prompted our family to pursue an adoption from Ethiopia. What we believed at the time was a single act of obedience led to us bringing home three orphaned siblings. One and a half years later, yet another threesome from Ethiopia would join our family. We are now a family of two parents and nine kids (for now) who are all sold out to live a life that is not our own—to truly be one family that will accomplish much for His kingdom, to be a family that God uses."

Heidi & Kirk Weimer
Parents of Bereket, Genet, Brandon, Bethlehem, Isabella, Selam, Ambaw, Justice, and Bizuneh

CONTENTS

THE FAMILY GOD USES

FOREWORD BY DR. HENRY BLACKABY

From eternity God planned and purposed the family. Each family is to be available for God's purposes in their day, and every person in a family is important to God. In addition, each person in a family is to assist every other member of the family to know God intimately and respond to God's purposes. Therefore, the standard and measure for each family is crucial, beginning with the father. God touched Abram and through him touched all the succeeding generations. The covenant God made with Abram He then made with Isaac (Gen. 22:15-18; 26:1-5). Throughout the rest of Scripture, God makes reference to "Abraham, Isaac, and Jacob"! Later we encounter Joseph and his family, then David and all his family. The focus and purposes of God's activity rest on the generations. It seems that when God calls and touches one man, He is purposing to call and work through his succeeding generations.

I have always been aware of this pattern in my own life and family and have endeavoured to live a godly life in my family and before each member of our family. We have been given four sons and one daughter. Each has married, adding five more "adult children" to our family, and each one of them is very special to us. From these married children God has granted us 14 grandchildren (seven boys and seven girls). What a challenge and a joy to be the "father" to 26 of us, knowing God has a special purpose for each of them and that my life is vital to each of them as they come to know God and His purposes for their life.

God has given us wonderful ways to help encourage one another over the years.

1. One of my principles was to include our family in our ministry. Over the years our children helped with ushering, childcare, sound systems, choir directing, missions committees, youth groups, college ministry, and church planting, to mention a few things. This involvement helped them see the value of investing in kingdom ministry and allowed us to rejoice together when the fruit of our labor began to grow.

2. We did our best to gather around the kitchen table every day for meals. This time was invaluable as we shared our days together and heard what was going on in one another's lives.

3. We shared our "spiritual markers" with our children so they knew the times when God touched and changed us as a family. One of our children shared with me, "Dad, we don't think that you knew how close we have come to falling away from God. But when the temptations came, we thought of you and Mom and how God has led you and our family, and we just could not do it." I was so glad that I had shared God's work in our family with them.

4. I constantly shared with our children, "Give God your best! He is God and deserves nothing less than our best!" I did not urge them to higher education, but all five earned degrees from both university and seminary. The four boys all have earned doctor's degrees from seminaries, and all of my children and their spouses continue to serve God and His people.

5. We have sponsored a family reunion every other year to bring all our children and grandchildren together. Sometimes we have been able to meet in some pretty amazing places. We also try to gather as a family on special days throughout the year to help them connect with one another and share about what God is doing in their lives.

6. I have deliberately chosen to write books with each of my five children, introducing them to communicating God's truths through books. I wanted to give them the incentive to write on their own long after I am gone.

7. I have had the privilege of speaking with each of our children in various conference settings and listened carefully to them as they shared. They have all learned to communicate our "family" message to others in their own unique ways, and they do so quite effectively. We are always amazed at what God does through people who put their lives completely into His hands and humbled as God continues to give our family members opportunities to write and proclaim His message around the world.

Our own family has been tremendously important to Marilynn and me, but our church families over the years have been no less important. Serving with God's people has been an absolute thrill over these past 50 years of ministry. I have always said God's people are the best people in the world, and God has allowed me the privilege of serving with some of His finest servants.

Tom is my second-oldest son. His journey with God has taken him in different directions than my other children. He has served God in several capacities over the years, and he and Kim have had unique opportunities to serve the Lord with their family in several countries. They lived overseas for seven years, serving God's people in an international church comprised of those in the international business community and the military. Living internationally provides valuable insights into what it means to be family as well as unique challenges in keeping a family strong while living in a foreign language and culture.

In the Scriptures God uses families. We are so grateful that He is still using ours and know He will use your family in incredible ways, too!

—Dr. Henry T. Blackaby

ABOUT THE AUTHORS

KIM BLACKABY

Kim Blackaby began her spiritual journey at age 15 in Faith Baptist Church where her pastor was Henry T. Blackaby. She saw firsthand the principles of *Experiencing God* in action and just what a big God can do with a small congregation. After receiving her Bachelors of Education from the University of Saskatchewan, she was involved in church planting in a small town where she taught school. Since marrying Tom, she has served as a pastor's wife in three churches, including seven years in an international congregation in Stavanger, Norway. She has been instrumental in developing prayer and women's ministries, leading children's musicals and women's Bible studies, and serving on the worship team as vocalist and accompanist. Kim and Tom have three great children and live near Vancouver, British Columbia, Canada.

DR. TOM BLACKABY

Tom was born in California but grew up in Saskatoon, Saskatchewan, Canada, where his father Henry T. Blackaby pastored Faith Baptist Church and developed the material for *Experiencing Go* He holds a Bachelors of Education from the University of Saskatchewan, a Master of Divinity from Southwestern Baptist Theological Seminary, and a Doctor of Ministry from Golden Gate Baptist Theological Seminary. Tom has served as Associate Pastor of music/youth/education in four churches and seven years as Senior Pastor of North Sea Baptist Church in Stavanger, Norway. He served four years as National Worship Consultant for the Canadian National Baptist Convention and currently serves as Director of International Ministries for Blackaby Ministries International. Tom has coauthored *The Man God Uses* (trade book, youth edition, devotional journal), *Anointed to Be God's Servants*, *The Blackaby Study Bible*, and *Encounters with God Daily Bible* as well as written devotional articles for *HomeLife* magazine for four years.

INTRODUCTION

When we began to write this book, Kim and I were slightly reticent—not because we did not believe in it, for we are convinced God uses families all the time in His kingdom, but because we didn't want to appear as if we are putting our own Blackaby family as examples of how families ought to do things. Certainly God has used my father in very significant ways to bless and encourage millions of people through his book, *Experiencing God: Knowing and Doing the Will of God*, and yes, each of the members in our family is serving the Lord in various capacities. But this project is not really about us. It is about God and what He can accomplish through His people. We examined the larger Blackaby family as well as other relatives who have contributed to our desire to know and to serve God. It is humbling to see how influential and inspirational they have been to us over the years. We also are keenly aware of how God is using many other families around the world today in amazingly creative capacities. Even though we give examples from our family background describing some of the principles we have sought to live by, we also include many other wonderful families' journeys with God that will encourage and inspire you.

In this book we will walk together through the Bible looking at many different families and how God chose to use them in various ways. Some were chosen to raise children He was going to use later in life, others God chose to become families of influence through which He would impact many lives, and still others were invited to be faithful in simple tasks that God had prepared for them. We will share biblical truths and principles in this book and provide opportunities for you to examine your own family and your own walk with God. Exercises will help you look more closely at how God has designed your family for ministry and service, and ideas will spark your imagination for what God may have in store for you, your children, and relatives in serving in God's kingdom.

Parents, the activities we included are simply suggestions of how you might teach your family members some important truths. You are not expected to do all of them. Rather, select those you feel are appropriate, modify them, or come up with your own ideas of how to share important principles and truths with your children.

Please understand that this book is not intended to lay guilt trips on God's people. It is written with the hope of inspiring families to see the amazing possibilities for how each one can intentionally be a family of influence wherever God has placed them. Work through this book prayerfully seeking the heart and mind of God. Listen carefully to what the Holy Spirit may be revealing to you about how He wants to draw your family closer together to be a light in your neighborhood and world. Our prayer is that you will come to experience God in your family as you seek and serve Him together and that your family will become one of influence that leaves a legacy of faithfulness for the next generations to follow.

We're grateful to the amazing members of North Sea Baptist Church, Stavanger, Norway, for being family to us for seven great years, to the members of First Baptist Church, Biloxi, Mississippi, for their inspiration in all they do to help families be families of influence in their community and around the world, and to thousands of churches and ministries internationally who serve God in places where the cost to families is much higher than most people ever know.

Go even deeper in your study with our NewHope book that was the basis for this study and that includes end-of-chapter reflections: *The Family God Uses: Leaving a Legacy of Influence* (ISBN 78-1-59669-251-0).

ABOUT THE STUDY

Get ready. You are about to embark on a journey. This journey will take you and your family to places to which you've never been. From time to time along the path, you may experience some rocky terrain, confusing forks in the road, and frustrating obstacles. But without question you will experience sights and sounds that you could only dream of. Welcome to the journey to becoming *The Family God Uses*.

HOW TO USE THIS BOOK

We recognize that more varieties of families exist today than quite possibly any other time in history. From traditional families consisting of a mom, a dad, two kids, and a dog to a single mom raising three kids, and from step-families to grandparents raising their grandchildren, families look very different. In addition, families are busier than ever. But, no matter what your family's structure or schedules look like, *The Family God Uses* is for you. Here are a few different use plans that could fit with your family's lifestyle. You may even wish to customize them to fit your needs.

Family Disciple-Making Guide Many resources can give you philosophy for raising kids or serving together. However, *The Family God Uses* is a comprehensive resource for helping you not only grow as an individual but also to pass what you are learning on to the rest of your family.

Here's what to do. As you read each chapter, you will be challenged to pause and discuss an idea with your spouse or children (see components on p. 11). When God teaches you a truth, re-teach it to your family. Don't feel rushed. Take all the time you need to do this. Some will finish very quickly. Others will take months just to complete one chapter. That's OK. It's important that you each grasp what God is saying before you move on to the next concept. Have conversations, follow-up conversations, and reinforcement conversations. Take the time to pray through ideas and concepts as a family, then go live out that truth together as you become a home of influence in your neighborhood and community.

Daily Bible Study You may also choose to use this book for your daily quiet time or Bible study. That's a great idea! Instead of dividing each chapter into individual days, chapters are divided into short, manageable sections. Our recommendation is that you interact with one or two sections per day depending on what your schedule permits.

Group Bible Study One of the greatest ways to experience all this study has to offer is to be involved in a small group of *The Family God Uses*. Walking through this journey with other families will energize and motivate you along the way. You may choose to start a new group in your church or use this study in an existing small group or Sunday School class. You might even decide to pull together some families in your neighborhood or from your child's soccer team. Whatever you choose, the seven-week small group Bible study guide beginning on page 148 will help you get started and facilitate your group.

COMPONENTS OF EACH CHAPTER

Each chapter of *The Family God Uses* has multiple components and features designed with you in mind to help you as you journey toward becoming a home of influence.

Bringing It Home

One of the most difficult yet most important tasks God has given parents is to help children grow in their faith. Sometimes, it is a challenge to know what to do and when to do it. This feature will provide you with ideas for bringing truth from God's Word home to your family. Here, you will also find simple and practical ideas for mobilizing your family to do ministry together.

Use the activities suggested in this section if you'd like. You may find that some activities don't work for your family, and that's fine. Adapt them. Make them your own. Or, allow them to be a catalyst for other ideas.

From Our Family to Yours

In Titus 2, the apostle Paul speaks of the value of someone who is older in the faith speaking into the lives of those who are younger. From Our Family to Yours gives Tom and Kim the opportunity to share some things that they have seen God do in and through their family over the years.

One Family's Story

From the Genesis to Revelation, God's Word is packed with truth that teaches us how to become families God uses. Many times, though, it is tough to grasp those truths until we see them fleshed out in real stories of real families God has used. One Family's Story shows how real families live out biblical principles in real-life situations.

Unlocking Your Influence

What will you do now? By taking the principles you learn in this study to heart and re-teaching them to your family, you will begin to become a home of influence among your friends, extended families, and neighbors. Unlocking Your Influence gives you thought-provoking questions to ponder and challenging topics to discuss with your spouse as you work together to unlock your family's influence.

Chapter 1

GOD'S DESIGN FOR FAMILIES

Every society down through the ages has families recognized by all as families of influence. Some are extremely wealthy and powerful. Some have provided employment to thousands for generations. Some families have a long line of members involved in politics or crime. Others are of royal lineage or influence through academics, art, entertainment, or social reform. These families often pass their influence, wealth, or power to future generations. Their influence can extend decades if not centuries. Yet, none have had more of an impact than those God has used.

You may choose to engage this chapter for a week or two. Or, maybe because of your family's hectic schedule, it will take you a month or more. That's OK. Don't rush it. Your journey to becoming a home of influence is just as important as your destination. So, take all the time you need to interact with your spouse and your kids as together you discover God's design for families.

GETTING STARTED

The Bible reveals that God has used families to impact mankind. They have carried out His will, obeyed His commands, led faithful lives, and become integral to God's strategy for redeeming lost humanity. But the good news is that these families were not particularly extraordinary. Most were not of royal descent or of great wealth and power. In fact, the families God used were flawed just like mine and yours. But two things set them apart from other families: their ability to hear God and their willingness to obey Him.

Maybe you read that and think, "I've never heard God speak before." Our prayer is that as you embark on your journey through this study, you and your family will begin to recognize where He is working in your very own spheres of influence and then join Him in that work.

We are excited about what God will show you over the next several weeks or months. It's important to remember that this Bible study journey is not just for you. It's for your entire family. To help you as you grow, serve, and learn together, throughout the study we have provided a host of practical ideas such as activities, games, service opportunities, and discussion starters in a feature called Bringing It Home. Here's one to get you started.

> " The families God used were flawed just like mine and yours. "

Bringing It Home
→ Ideas your family can use today ←

Child—Help your child draw a picture of his family or cut out magazine pictures that make him think of them (such as a flower mom likes, a car for dad, a basketball for brother, and so forth) and paste them on a piece of paper. Have him write or tell you one thing that is special about each family member.

Teen—Send your teen a text that says something like, "I think you're cool because ..." (Be careful not to be too cheesy.)

Adults—Write down any prayers or commitments you have made to God regarding your family from when you were married or first had children.

All Together—Discuss as a family, "What is the best thing about our family?"

At the end of each day of creation, God looked at what He had just created and saw that it was good. He saw the light and said it was good. After calling the dry land earth and gathering the waters into seas, He said that it was good. Then He created the plants and saw that was good. Then God saw everything that He had made and recognized indeed it was very good.

[You can find the creation account in Genesis 1:1-31.]

Read Genesis 2:18.

> The LORD God said, "It is not good that man should be alone; I will make him a helper comparable to him."
> GENESIS 2:18

1. What do you notice that is intriguing about God's reaction to what He had just created?

While God was talking with Adam, He realized there was a problem. All the creatures had companions to interact with except Adam. "The LORD God said, [for the first time] 'It is not good that the man should be alone. I will make a suitable helper for him'" (Gen. 2:18).

From that time on, a family was established. Consider for a moment the difference between humankind and the rest of creation. Some animals bond for life or group together for protection and community, but no other creatures have such life-long bonds characterized by deep sacrificial relationships as humankind. It is important to understand that humankind was not created simply to procreate and subdue the earth. Rather, we were created for something much larger. We'll think about that in the next section.

GOD'S PURPOSES FOR THE FAMILY

COMPANIONSHIP

According to Genesis 2:18, God saw Adam had a need that other creatures could not address. So God created Eve, and together Adam and Eve became inseparable, for good and bad! They walked with God together, sinned against God together, were cast out of the garden of Eden together, and had children together. Companionship is a primary aspect of family that should never be underestimated. We were never meant to be alone. We need each other.

Each Christmas our family traditionally sits down, hot cider and snacks in hand, and shares how God answered prayer in our family life that year. Accepting our current ministry position involved moving back to Canada from Norway. We sat down together as a family and talked about what God was doing in our lives. We talked about how God had been working in our hearts, giving us a sense that He was about to change our focus. Then we asked the children what they sensed God was telling them. Together as a family we chose to accept the new adventure God had for us.

Noah persevered for many years in a very lonely task. I doubt he could have accomplished it without his family at his side. Our families can support and encourage us in our obedience to God even if others misunderstand us. Companionship is important in God's plan for His people. In fact, it is one of the Holy Spirit's primary roles for members in God's family. Christ Himself promised that He would never leave us (John 14:16; Heb. 13:5)!

1. Pause now and thank God for the life, love, and laughter your family finds in God-given companionship. You may write your prayer here.

[The Greek word to describe the Holy Spirit is parakletos, meaning comforter, companion, counselor, or advocate.]

TRAINING

Families are God's training ground. Children learn the fundamentals of building strong relationships in the home. The family is the perfect place to learn about love, trust, respect for others, sharing, honoring one another, obeying authority, working together, sacrifice, carrying out responsibilities, integrity, honesty, grace, hard work, prayer, commitment, values, and much more.

1. Many Christians find a correlation between their relationship with their earthly dad and their heavenly Father. Based on your or your spouse's actions, what are your children being trained to believe about God? Mark all that apply.

○ He's harsh and judgemental.
○ He expects more of me than I can deliver.
○ I'm never good enough for Him.

○ He's forgiving.
○ He's kind and generous.
○ Other: _____

God looks for parents who seek Him to help their children have a proper and healthy view of who He is. Although dysfunctional homes may cause children to run from the God their parents claim to serve, others come to know and love God very early because their homes are filled with loving parents who offer grace, compassion, trust, and a quiet strength that cause them to draw near to God. When God has access to the parents' hearts, the home becomes a wonderful place where God is honored and where children and their friends are drawn into His presence.

Bringing It Home
→ Ideas your family can use today ←

Child—Name three things each member of your family has taught you to do.

Teen—What are the most important things your parents have taught you? How are parents portrayed in television sitcoms and movies? Can you think of an example of parents (real-life or actors) who were good teachers?

Adult—List the five most important things you believe a child needs to learn at home. Complete this separately from your spouse and then compare lists. What have you intentionally done to teach your children these five things?

All Together—Share with each other or act out what you have learned from your other family members.

[Parents, here are some suggested discussion starters to help the whole family begin to see how they are doing in God's training ground.]

PROTECTION

Families have an innate sense to protect one another. Every child knows that is what big brothers or big sisters are for! Parents "go to bat" for their children in schools, athletics, and other aspects of life because of our deep bonds. Later the tables are turned, and the children begin to care for aging parents, finding suitable accommodations for them or taking their parents into their homes to care for and protect them.

Families protect one another against those who would harm, abuse, or cheat them. They seek to prevent illness by providing medical attention when needed and to counsel against making unwise choices. The old phrase "blood is thicker than water" recognizes the bond that family members have and the sacrifices they are willing to make for one another.

My father remembers vividly an incident at one of our high school soccer games. Three of his sons were playing, and an opposing player tackled the youngest with unnecessary force. Within minutes, that player was introduced to the two older and stronger brothers who delivered a rather strong (and legal) message of caution should he consider hurting their little brother again.

IN THE COMMUNITY

Not only was the family created for companionship and training, but it was also created for community impact. The family is the foundation for every community. In the family we learn to be productive members of society. Where communities have a strong sense of responsibility toward one another, care for one another's children, and respect others' property, there is a real sense of *we* and *ours* rather than *me* and *mine*. Crime rates are lower where strong family values exist. Vandalism is lower where good community programs and sports clubs support families, and property theft is drastically reduced where a strong sense of community grows. People watch out for one another when family values are taught and lived out.

Bringing It Home

→ Ideas your family can use today ←

[How can your family begin to impact your community? Here are a few ideas.]

Child—Tell your child, "On your way home from school, try to pick up 10 pieces of trash along the way." Be sure to talk about how that task made him feel.

Teen—Encourage your teen to offer to help a neighbor, to clean or repaint a wall or fence marred by graffiti, or maybe even to volunteer at a local children's sports event.

Adult—Consider being a block parent; intentionally stand outside your home when children return from school; think about neighborhood latch-key children and consider what you might do to help.

All Together—Find a park near your home where you can go to pick up trash together or offer to pull weeds, trim hedges, or do basic maintenance for an elderly person.

IN THE KINGDOM OF GOD

The family is a picture of God's eternal family. It is fascinating to see how God often alluded to family when describing Himself, His kingdom, and His people. Here are a few of those instances.

- "My house shall be called a house of prayer" (Matt. 21:13).
- "Our Father who art in heaven …" (Matt. 6:9, ASV).
- "As many as received Him, to them He gave the right to become children of God, to those who believe in His name" (John 1:12).
- "The Spirit Himself bears witness with our spirit that we are children of God, and if children, then heirs—heirs of God and joint heirs with Christ, if indeed we suffer with Him, that we may also be glorified together" (Rom. 8:16-17).
- "In My Father's house are many mansions; if it were not so, I would have told you. I go to prepare a place for you" (John 14:2).
- "Whoever does the will of My Father in heaven is My brother and sister and mother" (Matt. 12:50).
- "For this reason I bow my knees to the Father of our Lord Jesus Christ, from whom the whole family in heaven and earth is named" (Eph. 3:14-15).

When the disciples asked Jesus to teach them to pray, He could have taught them to address God in many different ways: God of Heaven and Earth, Almighty Creator, Holy One of Israel. Or He could have used any of God's Old Testament names such as Banner, Healer, Provider, and Lord God. Instead, He chose to have them approach God with the most intimate term: *Father*.

1. What thoughts come to mind as you view God through the lens of your own father?

[The Greek word normally translated father also includes the meanings of a male ancestor, parent, and guardian. On many occasions God demonstrated a parent's care toward His people as well as a guardian's protection from their enemies.]

We know that Jesus introduced God as Heavenly Father in His Sermon on the Mount (see Matt. 5:16,45,48; 6:1,4), but we don't know if Christ's disciples had ever considered addressing Almighty Creator, all-powerful God as Father before. When Jesus taught His disciples to pray, He did more than model a spiritual discipline. He helped them understand the kind of relationship God wants to have with us. You would be hard-pressed to find any other religion that offers such an intimate relationship with God—a Creator who is above and beyond all human comprehension yet who desires to have the same type of relationship a father has to his children.

IN THE CHURCH

The family is a picture of how the local church is to function. Just as every child was intended to be born into a family, so every new believer is born into the kingdom of God and into a community of faith, a local church.

The church is designed to be family to fellow believers who nurture and care for each other as family members care for one another. In the church new believers grow and mature. Everyone learns about the fundamentals of faith and belief in God, and each one contributes by using their gifts and abilities for the betterment of all. Strong families make a strong church, and a strong church strengthens families and equips them to participate together in God's kingdom. Many Christians have forgotten that God has expectations for His people. They come to God as they are and on their own terms. Yet the Bible tells us that God set the requirements for what was acceptable in His presence. Many times God rejected what was offered to Him in worship and sacrifice because it did not meet His standards or requirements. God also has expectations for His people regarding their home life.

> Train up a child in the way he should go, even when he is old he will not depart from it.
> PROVERBS 22:6, NASB

Look at Proverbs 22:6 above. Some people have taken this verse to be a promise from God when in actuality it is a principle to follow. This verse is not providing a guarantee, but a principle, a guideline for parents to follow as they raise their children. It may be that children will depart from the Lord for a time, but the teachings will never depart from them!

The Old Testament was God's training ground for His people and an opportunity for them to develop godly habits in their homes, in their relationships with people, and in their worship of God. But over and over they chose to follow other priorities, worldly values, and secular morals. They abandoned God's ways in their homes, businesses, and worship. God tried to protect His people from these choices because He knew their consequences for families, children, and their way of life.

From Our Family to Yours

[My sister, Carrie, tells how the influence of our parents has impacted her life.]

"My parents' steadfast and complete trust in Christ impacted me as a child. They confronted many challenges through the years, and each was met with the confidence that God would help them through—and He did. The same God who was faithful to my parents is the same God who is now faithful to me and my family as we serve on the mission field. Having absolute confidence of God's presence and knowing our lives are in His hands has carried us through many trials. It is my hope that our children both see and experience what it means to fully trust in the Lord and His faithfulness."—**Carrie Blackaby Webb**

Unlocking Your Influence

As you finish this section, *consider this...*

1. How often do you discuss spiritual things with your children or with your spouse?

[**Pause now to prayerfully consider these questions. Discuss them with your spouse as you discover together how to unlock your family's influence.**]

2. How much do you depend on Sunday School teachers, youth leaders, or pastors to teach your family about God rather than doing it yourself?

3. What is one thing you can do to begin to talk about spiritual things with your children or spouse?

GOD'S DESIGN FOR FAMILY LIFE

The Jewish family model is rooted in long-standing traditions, close family ties, and maintaining good standing with neighbors. Family lines have always been important to God's people, so much so that Christ's lineage is given in both Matthew and Luke to demonstrate His legitimacy as the Messiah. Where a person's family came from and to whom they were related often meant life or death. It also opened doors of opportunity to influence others.

Families are so important to God that He provides guidance and safeguards throughout Scripture to protect them. The Books of Leviticus and Deuteronomy are essentially manuals to help the people love the Lord their

God with all their heart, soul, strength, and mind and to love their neighbor as themselves.

1. Read Exodus 20:1-17 in your Bible. Which commandments seem to apply most to family life? How do you think they are beneficial to the family?

Look closely at the fifth commandment in Exodus 20:12.

> "Honor your father and your mother, that your days may be long upon the land which the LORD your God is giving you."
> EXODUS 20:12

2. How do you think this commandment protects and preserves the family?

Now read Exodus 20:14.

> "You shall not commit adultery."
> EXODUS 20:14

3. What effects on society occur because of a disregard for this seventh commandment? Parents, what measures are you taking (or could you take) to ensure that an adulterous relationship doesn't destroy your family?

Read Exodus 20:17.

> "You shall not covet your neighbor's house; you shall not covet your neighbor's wife, nor his male servant, nor his female servant, nor his ox, nor his donkey, nor anything that is your neighbor's."
> EXODUS 20:17

4. In the tenth commandment, God gives examples of things not to be coveted. What does it mean to covet? How could a covetous attitude negatively affect a family?

One Family's Story

Barton Priebe is an unusual pastor who serves in a mega-city. By all accounts he is a great preacher and a well-organized, godly man who is passionate about helping God's people live authentic Christianity. He devoutly believes in a man leading his family in worship and encourages his church members to do so. This may not be unusual, but his heritage is. Barton's father faithfully pastored churches 30 years and then became a chaplain in a senior's housing complex. His grandfather was a construction worker and lay-pastor who preached in small churches sharing the truths of the Bible. His great-grandfather was an itinerate evangelist who canvassed the prairies of Canada preaching the gospel. But that is not all. His brother is a missionary to an unreached tribe in Tanzania. His uncle and aunt were missionaries in Kenya for 20 years and now serve in Canada.

Barton cannot remember his parents ever pressuring any of their three children to go into the ministry. In fact, they were more likely to discourage it because of the challenges and hardships pastors' families face. But their passion for Christ and love for God's people was so contagious that all three of their children serve the Lord and married wives who love the Lord. Together they support their churches.

[**Passion for Christ and love for God's people can be contagious.**]

5. Considering the previous story, what kind of heritage do you desire for your children? What things can you do to help leave that kind of legacy?

Read Deuteronomy 6:1-9,12-13.

"Now this is the commandment, and these are the statutes and judgments which the LORD your God has commanded to teach you, that you may observe them in the land which you are crossing over to possess, that you may fear the LORD your God, to keep all His statutes and His commandments which I command you, you and your son and your grandson, all the days of your life, and that your days may be prolonged. Therefore hear, O Israel, and be careful to observe it, that it may be well with you, and that you may multiply greatly as the LORD God of your fathers has promised you—'a land flowing with milk and honey.' Hear, O Israel: The LORD our God, the LORD is one! You shall love the LORD your God with all your heart, with all your soul, and with all your strength. And these words which I command you today shall be in your heart. You shall teach them diligently to your children, and shall talk of them when you sit in your house, when you walk by the way, when you lie down, and when you rise up. You shall bind them as a sign on your hand, and they shall be as frontlets between your eyes. You shall write them on the doorposts of your house and on your gates. ... Beware, lest you forget the LORD who brought you out of the land of Egypt, from the house of bondage. You shall fear the LORD your God and serve Him, and shall take oaths in His name."

DEUTERONOMY 6:1-9,12-13

6. What does God expect of the family in relationship to Him?

The previous passage outlines God's strategy for His people to maintain their relationship with Him. This had a generational impact and allowed them to experience all that He planned for them. The key to this was the family. Let's explore God's expectations for the family.

DEMONSTRATE A LOVE RELATIONSHIP WITH GOD

A relationship with God will naturally work itself out in our daily actions before our children. We can demonstrate our love for Him by following His commands, through our worship, and in seeking time with Him. We further demonstrate our love by remaining faithful through the years, never denying God, and trusting Him to be faithful to do what He promised. When our children watch our lives, they should have no doubt that we love God (see Deut. 6:5).

1. What are some ways you express your love to God?

KNOW GOD'S WORD

Read Psalm 119:11. More than repetition, knowing His Word means allowing it to wash over our lives and become a part of who we are.

> **Your word I have hidden in my heart, that I might not sin against You.**
> PSALM 119:11

1. To what degree would you say you are familiar with God's Word?

- ◯ Not at all familiar
- ◯ Fairly familiar
- ◯ I know one or two verses
- ◯ Very familiar

Bringing It Home
→ **Ideas your family can use today** ←

Child—Help your child design a poster using a verse you would like to memorize (for example, Deut. 6:4-5, GNB: "Israel, remember this! The LORD—and the LORD alone—is our God. Love the LORD your God with all your heart, with all your soul, and with all your strength").

Teen—Encourage your teen to choose two Bible verses to memorize and compete with your family for a prize at the end of the week. The prize could be things like a $20 gas card, a new shirt, or a trip to the mall. Be creative but not cheesy.

Adult—Use a small notebook or diary and begin to compile a list of faith-building Bible verses to share with your family members as the need arises.

All Together—Make a set of Bible verse cards to leave at the table where you eat. Bring them out at meal times to help one another remember the verses. Try to recall the verses by the reference and by key words. Several Web sites offer Scripture memory helps and ready-to-print Bible verse cards. Try *www.kidstalkaboutgod.org*; *www.memoryversecards.com*; *www.kidprintables.com/bibleverses*; or search online for other favorite sites.

TEACH AND APPLY GOD'S WORD

> "You shall teach them diligently to your children, and shall talk of them when you sit in your house, when you walk by the way, when you lie down, and when you rise up."
>
> DEUTERONOMY 6:7

God's Word is to be "carefully" (diligently, pointedly, intensively, purposefully) taught. Purposefully teaching God's truth to our children takes deliberate effort. Bible stories, family devotions, Sunday School, and Bible studies are some ways to do this. Having God so much a part of everything we do impresses upon the children that God has first place in their parents' lives.

God expects that parents will consult Him and His Word in everyday situations. Parents should include spiritual conversations in everyday life—as they walk along the road, greet their children in the morning, put children to bed at night, and put reminders in their homes. This shows great respect and regard for God's Word as being the trustworthy foundation for the family.

KEEP GOD'S WORD VISIBLE

[Belonging creates a sense of values, teaches acceptable behaviors, and gives purpose and meaning to people.]

Scripture in your home is an everyday reminder that God is a part of your family's identity. Probably the most important aspect of displaying Scripture is to help children know the Bible from an early age. Frame Scripture for the walls of your home, post it above doors, or stitch it into pillows to help create a sense of belonging in children.

1. When you walk into your home, what do you notice first? What prominence does God's Word have?

Bringing It Home
→ Ideas your family can use today ←

Child—Walk with your child around your house and count how many things remind you of God.

Teen—Ask your teen, "If you were to put one Bible verse prominently in your bedroom, which one would it be? When friends look around your room, what do they think is most important in your life?"

Adult—Talk with your spouse about how well your house reflects your heart for God.

All Together—Choose one Bible verse that represents your family or your heart for God, and find a way to place it visibly in or around your home.

REMEMBER GOD'S DEEDS

Remembering what God has done is a key to continually walking in faith and obedience. As we respond to God in obedience, we experience His faithfulness and blessing, deepening our trust in Him and our desire to follow Him.

1. Talk as a family about some times when God has answered a prayer or your family has experienced God's help.

In the Old Testament, God's people set up piles of stones as markers of special times of God's intervention. Take some time this week and collect some smooth stones with your family. Then write on those stones some specific times when God has answered a prayer, worked a miracle, or helped your family in a time of need. Place those stones in a prominent area in your house to remind you of God's deeds.

DEMONSTRATE REVERENCE, OBEDIENCE, AND SERVICE TO GOD

Think about the last time your family worshiped together. Did you sit together? It is important for your children to see you singing songs, putting money in the offering plate, and opening your Bible to read along at church. These are teaching tools that communicate reverence for God. Not using God's name in vain or in an empty fashion, following God's commands even when you do not feel like it, and going out of your way to help others in need indicate to our children how important our relationship with God is.

From Our Family to Yours

[Do you have a kicking-rock time with your children?]

While walking with my son on a familiar pathway that leads to his school, we take turns kicking a rock as far as possible. The challenge is to keep the rock from dropping off a bridge, falling down a grate, getting stuck under a car, or becoming lost in tall grass. With each kick, I talk to my son about his day, God's creation, how to be a good influence on his friends, and how to deal with bullies, and we pray about his life-challenges. We call it our kicking-rock time.

The best way to teach your children is to walk at their pace, helping them learn spiritual things at their level. Teachable moments are great for taking ordinary opportunities to intentionally explain God and the Christian life.

Jesus affirmed His Father's desire to protect the family in His teachings, particularly as He offered expanded versions of Old Testament teachings. Though He never married, He had high regard for the value of a man and woman coming together as one in marriage. In one particular exchange, Jesus affirmed marriage and discouraged divorce.

Read Mark 10:2-12.

" Out of respect for younger Christians in the faith, we can choose to take small steps through the Scripture so they can grow according to their ability and understanding. "
Dr. Jack McGorman

The Pharisees came and asked Him, "Is it lawful for a man to divorce his wife?" testing Him. And He answered and said to them, "What did Moses command you?" They said, "Moses permitted a man to write a certificate of divorce, and to dismiss her." And Jesus answered and said to them, "Because of the hardness of your heart he wrote you this precept. But from the beginning of the creation, God 'made them male and female.' 'For this reason a man shall leave his father and mother and be joined to his wife, and the two shall become one flesh'; so then they are no longer two, but one flesh. Therefore what God has joined together, let not man separate." In the house His disciples also asked Him again about the same matter. So He said to them, "Whoever divorces his wife and marries another commits adultery against her. And if a woman divorces her husband and marries another, she commits adultery."

MARK 10:2-12

1. Why did Jesus say what He did about divorce, even though it may seem somewhat strict or harsh?

Unlocking Your Influence

As you finish looking at truth, *consider this...*

1. What are some ways you can make God more of a priority within your home?

[Take some time to discuss these questions with your spouse before you move to the next section.]

2. What are some practical ideas that can help you better know and apply Scripture in your life?

3. Discuss a time in your week when you can have "kicking-rock time" with each of your children.

GOD'S FAMILIES THROUGHOUT SCRIPTURE

Some of the greatest models of the family are found in the Bible. Men and women who honored God and raised their children to walk in His ways had profound impact and influence on those around them.

We can see how individual families' influence continues to affect those who join their journey through the pages of Scripture.

ABRAHAM: A GODLY FATHER

Now let's take a closer look at a family God used. The biblical narrative tells us that:

- Abraham obeyed God the moment he was called out of his home country (Gen. 12:1).
- Abraham and Sarah stepped out in faith, left the comforts of civilized life, and became nomads, trusting that the God who called them would be true to His word.
- Abraham persevered through tough times, military conflict, enemy raids, and several international relocations; yet he remained faithful.
- Abraham honored God, grew in his relationship and understanding of God, took a stand for God, listened and prayed to God, and sought God throughout his life. Consequently, God blessed him tremendously.

[For further study, check out Ruth's impact, Joseph's saving a nation from starvation, and Daniel's influence in Babylon. (See the Book of Ruth, Genesis 30–47, and Daniel 1–12.)]

Isaac grew up in this home. As long as Abraham was faithful to the covenant relationship God made with him, Isaac enjoyed the same kind of covenant relationship with God that Abraham enjoyed. The covenant was renewed with Isaac. As Isaac was faithful, his son, Jacob, had the opportunity to have the same kind of covenant relationship with God.

1. Reflecting on the story of Abraham and Isaac, in what ways did Abraham model commitment and obedience? Refer in your Bible to Genesis 12:1-4; 15:1-6; 22:1-13.

We know about Abraham's faith journey with God before Isaac was born because Abraham told these stories to Isaac and they were passed down to succeeding generations and recorded. As a dad, Abraham modeled a devoted life. He did not say one thing in the presence of God and then go and do another before his family.

2. What are some other biblical examples of people who, because of their obedience, were used mightily by God?

3. Name some modern-day examples of people who have been used by God because of their devotion to Him.

Bringing It Home

→ Ideas your family can use today ←

Child—Play "follow the leader." Each person should take a turn either leading others around the house or doing actions others must copy. Discuss how it feels to "be in charge."

Teen—Who are the most influential people in your class? What makes them so influential? Is their influence on others positive or negative? Why?

Adult—Outside of your own family, whom are you influencing the most? How?

All Together—Name as a family people at your church who have various types of influence. Some may lead in worship, and others may be praying for people at home.

[Lead your family in a discussion of ways to be a positive influence on others. Here are a few discussion starters.]

One Family's Story

"We decided our family vacation had to have an impact on the poor, needy, and disadvantaged. We went to an impoverished area in Mexico where we served alongside local churches. We

[**Check in chapter 6 or on the Web at www.namb.net for mission ideas your family can consider.**]

performed skits and dances and presented the message of the gospel in interesting ways for both children and adults. And then we visited Disneyland for a few days on the way home!"
—**Schroeder Family**

4. In what practical ways can you and your family be involved in God's work around the world?

IMPACTING FUTURE GENERATIONS

God often chooses to use families and their succeeding generations as long as they remain faithful to Him. Exodus 29 gives God's instructions relating to the high priest's role and to those He chose to serve. It includes directives to Aaron's sons who would follow in their dad's footsteps. The role of the high priest was incredibly important. In fact, the children of Israel depended on his performing this office before God on their behalf. It is interesting to see how God chose to work through Aaron's family as a priestly order. Everything about them was to be dedicated to the Lord, and their whole lives were to be given to studying for and performing the acts of priests to the Lord God.

Read Exodus 29:19-21,29-30.

"Take the other ram—the ram used for dedication—and tell Aaron and his sons to put their hands on its head. Kill it, and take some of its blood and put it on the lobes of the right ears of Aaron and his sons, on the thumbs of their right hands and on the big toes of their right feet. Throw the rest of the blood against all four sides of the altar. Take some of the blood that is on the altar and some of the anointing oil, and sprinkle it on Aaron and his clothes and on his sons and their clothes. He, his sons, and their clothes will then be dedicated to me … Aaron's priestly garments are to be handed on to his sons after his death, for them to wear when they are ordained. The son of Aaron who succeeds him as priest and who goes into the Tent of my presence to serve in the Holy Place is to wear these garments for seven days."
EXODUS 29:19-21,29-30, GNB

1. How did Aaron's obedience to God affect his family?

Had Aaron ever abandoned God and his role as High Priest, God likely would have chosen another family through whom to speak to His people. How Aaron walked before the Lord determined the livelihood and ministry of the generations of his family that followed.

I often wonder what impact my response to God will have on my children and their future. And I wonder if I ever refused God and caused Him to remove His intended blessings from my children.

When Barton Priebe questioned dozens of pastors' kids about their experiences in church, he found two consistent responses. Those who had abandoned the church and stopped pursuing a relationship with God did so either because they perceived their pastor-father as a hypocrite who did not live out the principles he preached or as loving the church more than his children. Those who continued in church and pursued a relationship with God saw their parent's Christianity as genuine. They often shared in his ministry and developed a deep love for the church and God's people. They never built up resentment toward God and the church because their father maintained a good balance between family and ministry time. This can certainly apply to families who are not in full-time ministry as well.

Many of the families God uses come into His service only after God adequately prepares them ahead of time. God seems to allow a time of equipping, training, testing, and shaping before He invites them into larger responsibilities. What we do for God is not something we manufacture; it is something God reveals to us when we are ready. Then we respond to His invitations and watch Him accomplish what He intends to do through us.

[What impact will my response to God have on my children and their future?]

2. Talk with your spouse about how you want to lead your family to serve God. What do you need to do to get ready to accept God's invitation?

One Family's Story

"Our family left Texas to homestead in northern Alberta, Canada. In 1958 Mom was trying to get a message to Dad at his sheep camp on the Peace River flats. After riding several hours on a horse and winding down hills to the river cabin, Mom lost her way in the dark. Seeing a small kerosene lamp shining in the cabin's window, she called out to Dad. The man working for Dad heard her, came outside, and shouted back, telling her to wait for him to come and get her.

"The next morning, the hired man showed Mom why he stopped her. Only a short distance ahead was a cliff with a sharp drop off. Mom said the Lord spoke to her immediately and said, 'Louise, I brought you and Keith (Dad) to a place where you were to provide spiritual light, and you have been trying to put out that light by crying and wanting to go back to Texas.' He then told her, 'I am tried of your complaining about how hard it is, and I want it stopped.' After this encounter, she was a changed woman, a phenomenal wife and ministry partner to my father until death parted them in January 2002. Two of her sons became pastors in Canada, one worked for a national convention of churches, and the others serve as faithful Christian ranchers and businessmen. The legacy and impact of the family continues to this day."—**D.K. Hale**

[When a family honors God in their home, God can do some pretty amazing things through them.]

3. Make two columns below, one listing some of the changes the Hale family faced and the other listing challenges you are facing as a family.

4. If you were writing your family's story as the author relayed the Hale's, what would you say about your response to God's direction?

What God does at a national level through His people is just as significant to Him as what He does at a personal level, even as one family prays for their neighbors to come to Christ. God is not limited in what He can do through His people when they are available to Him and willing to obey.

Unlocking Your Influence

As you finish looking at truth, *consider this...*

1. Name some of the characteristics of biblical families that made them so influential for God.

2. Are there parts of your life that God may want you to sacrifice so that your family will have greater impact for Him?

3. Discuss with your spouse and write your response to the author's statement, "I often wonder what impact my response to God will have on my children and their future. And I wonder if I ever refused God and caused Him to remove His intended blessings from my children."

[**What impact will your response to God have on your children and their future?**]

4. What are some areas in your family where God may be calling you to join Him through deeds, acts of kindness, or service?

Chapter 2

GOD USED FAMILIES TO BUILD THE CHURCH

The church is more than mere religious association; we are family—brothers and sisters in Christ. The first chapter emphasized God's design and purpose for the family. Remember that God is our Father and His people are His family. Now let's look more closely at how the family concept was important in the New Testament and particularly to the church, the body of Christ.

A biblical pattern shows God searches for people whose hearts are sensitive toward Him and then draws them into various assignments He has for them. Often one of the requirements for His servants is that they be seen "righteous" or "just" in His eyes. To be used by God, parents who seek to follow God wholeheartedly must lead their family to do the same.

> For You, O LORD, will bless the righteous; With favor You will surround him as with a shield.
> PSALM 5:12

GOD USED CHRIST'S FAMILY

The New Testament begins with the story of a young couple, Joseph and Mary, learning they were to have a child through the miraculous intervention of God's Holy Spirit. God chose a humble, hard-working family to raise His Son. Immediate challenges required Joseph's quick action to ensure the survival of his young bride and their new Son. Without his simple faith and timely obedience to God, the life of the Messiah would have been in jeopardy (Matt. 2:16). This couple, with Jesus' younger brothers and sisters, nurtured Jesus and provided the security and love every child needs. Though the Bible gives little information about Jesus' relationship with His family, it does give us some very interesting details.

> So her husband Joseph, being a righteous man, and not wanting to disgrace her publicly, decided to divorce her secretly. But after he had considered these things, an angel of the Lord suddenly appeared to him in a dream, saying, "Joseph, son of David, don't be afraid to take Mary as your wife, because what has been conceived in her is by the Holy Spirit. She will give birth to a son, and you are to name Him Jesus, because He will save His people from their sins." Now all this took place to fulfill what was spoken by the Lord through the prophet: See, the virgin will become pregnant and give birth to a son, and they will name Him Immanuel, which is translated "God is with us." When Joseph got up from sleeping, he did as the Lord's angel had commanded him. He married her but did not know her intimately until she gave birth to a son. And he named Him Jesus.
>
> MATTHEW 1:19-25, HCSB

1. What does Matthew 1:19-25 tell you about the kind of man Joseph was?

2. How does his reaction to the encounter with the angel also verify Joseph's character?

Now read Luke 1:28.

> And the angel came to her and said, "Rejoice, favored woman!
> The Lord is with you."
> Luke 1:28, HCSB

3. How does the angel describe Mary?

Both Joseph and Mary honored God even before they were married. The Bible describes Joseph as a righteous man (Matt. 1:19). That was his reputation in the community. He was kind and honorable, initially not wanting to embarrass or cause Mary public disgrace in breaking off the engagement. His willingness to follow God's direction to marry Mary demonstrated courage and fear of the Lord, as it would change the direction of his life and bring him tremendous responsibility.

Mary also sought after God. The angel describes her as "favored" and said "the Lord is with you" (Luke 1:28). Even though she was young, she demonstrated incredible humility and responsiveness to God as well as great courage to accept an incredible assignment from Him. I can't imagine what went through her heart later as she began to come to grips with how the course of events was leading her firstborn Son to a Roman cross.

Joseph and Mary were individually exemplary in their lives. Together they were just what God was looking for in a couple to parent His Son. They were both in a place spiritually to clearly discern God's voice and immediately obey God's directions regardless of the cost.

4. Discuss the manner in which Mary and Joseph heard from God. How can you hear and discern God's voice for yourself and your family?

5. How would you respond if God asked you to do something hard or costly? Is your relationship such that you would not hesitate to obey?

Without question God had encountered Joseph and Mary, and there was no question about what they had been asked to do. Imagine the stories they told Jesus while He was growing up about God's intervention in their lives and how God faithfully protected and led them through dangerous times.

Some of Jesus' other relatives also encountered God. An angel visited two of Jesus' older relatives even before His mother's encounter.

Read Luke 1:5-7,11-13.

> In the days of King Herod of Judea, there was a priest of Abijah's division named Zechariah. His wife was from the daughters of Aaron, and her name was Elizabeth. Both were righteous in God's sight, living without blame according to all the commandments and requirements of the Lord. But they had no children because Elizabeth could not conceive, and both of them were well along in years. … An angel of the Lord appeared to him, standing to the right of the altar of incense. When Zechariah saw him, he was startled and overcome with fear. But the angel said to him: Do not be afraid, Zechariah, because your prayer has been heard. Your wife Elizabeth will bear you a son, and you will name him John.
> LUKE 1:5-7,11-13, HCSB

6. What does Luke 1:5-7,11-13 say about the relationship that Zechariah and Elizabeth had with God?

Read Luke 1:17.

> "He will also go before Him in the spirit and power of Elijah, 'to turn the hearts of the fathers to the children,' and the disobedient to the wisdom of the just, to make ready a people prepared for the Lord."
> LUKE 1:17

7. What was significant about their child in relation to Jesus?

When God looked for a couple who could raise this important prophet, Elizabeth and Zechariah seemed most qualified. Luke 1:6 says, "Both were righteous in God's sight, living without blame according to all the commandments and requirements of the Lord."

As we look at Joseph, Mary, Zechariah, and Elizabeth, it seems that when God has in mind to work through families, He first looks for those who are already seeking Him! In some ways, God rewards a family for their faithfulness by working through them. God likely would not choose to work through those who ignore Him or who choose to go in their own directions rather than to seek God and His heart's desire for their lives. God seeks to work through families who have a relationship with Him.

From Our Family to Yours

The spiritual and physical lights were about to go out in a little church in Saskatoon, Canada, but what people saw and what God saw were two different things. People saw a flat-roofed, white-stuccoed building with a massive crack down the side, a front door that wouldn't open all the way because the overhang drooped too low, and only a few people who ventured inside. But God had an assignment in mind for a willing family who would come to that little church. God saw more than the 13 people gathered together each week to pray. He saw a future Bible college, dozens of mission church plants, hundreds of people being called into ministry, and a book called *Experiencing God.* But it depended on whether the family He chose would be faithful to the task and trust Him even when things looked bleak and discouraging.

> [God called our family to be faithful to His plans for our church in Saskatoon.]

God has prepared many such opportunities for those who are willing to serve. God is looking for those who are willing to work as greeters, stock the church's coffee bar, help weekly with a handicapped child, or a thousand other things. Individuals who are willing to serve can make a tremendous difference in the lives of others.

8. In what ways are you and your family already involved in serving God?

9. Do you feel as if God may want to use you in other areas of service? How?

Bringing It Home

→ **Ideas your family can use today** ←

Child—Help your child make a family tree going back as far as you can remember. Put a cross beside each person who is a Christian or who attends church. Lead your child in a prayer thanking God for putting him in your family.

Teen—Encourage your teen to write a note, e-mail, or text message to say "thank you" to a relative who has had a positive influence on him.

Adults—Think about the people in your church who do not have immediate family nearby. How can your family begin to "be family" to others? Plan to invite them home for a meal or holiday, or remember them on their birthdays.

All Together—Talk together and decide on a family who has children similar in age to yours to invite to do an activity with your family (such as hike, barbecue, or go bowling).

Unlocking Your Influence

As you finish looking at truth, *consider this ...*

1. How would people describe your family? Would they describe you based on your faith and obedience to God?

2. Recall a situation where you have seen God at work and you joined Him.

3. Think of people around you, whether at work, school, or church who have emotional, physical, or spiritual needs. How does God want to use your family to help meet those needs?

GOD USED JESUS' EXTENDED FAMILY

Some people are surprised when they realize that several of Jesus' relatives were very much a part of His ministry. They were instrumental in establishing the community of believers that came together after His resurrection and ascension. Mary followed Jesus' ministry from the very beginning right to the bitter end. Tradition says she became an important part of the church in Ephesus together with the apostle John, who was possibly her nephew.

Read John 1:29.

> The next day John saw Jesus coming toward him and said, "Here is the Lamb of God, who takes away the sin of the world!"
> JOHN 1:29, HCSB

1. Christ's cousin John the Baptist actually baptized Jesus in the Jordan River. What did John say about Jesus in John 1:29?

Jesus' half-brothers James and Jude wrote two New Testament books (see Gal. 1:19; Luke 6:16; Matt. 13:55). Many believe the disciples James and John, the sons of Zebedee, could have been His first cousins through their mother Salome who is thought to be Mary's sister (John 19:25; Matt. 27:56). This may explain why Salome would ask Jesus for special privileges for her two boys.

Read Matthew 20:20-21.

> Then the mother of Zebedee's sons approached Him with her sons. She knelt down to ask Him for something. "What do you want?" He asked her. "Promise," she said to Him, "that these

two sons of mine may sit, one on Your right and the other on Your left, in Your kingdom."

MATTHEW 20:20-21, HCSB

2. Why do you think Salome made this request of Jesus?

3. What does her request reveal about her understanding of who Jesus was?

Having family around Him would have been a great support to Jesus of Nazareth. Perhaps this gives insight into why James and John were two of His closest disciples and why He spoke so highly of John the Baptist (Matt. 11:11). Notice that cousins James, John, and John the Baptist and half-brothers Jude and James supported Christ as the Messiah. No one would have known Jesus better than His own family, and their acknowledgment of Christ's resurrection and ascension carries a great deal of weight historically.

From Our Family to Yours

One of my great joys has been to minister with my older brother, once as his associate pastor and currently in Blackaby Ministries International where I also serve alongside my father. A special bond exists between family members who know each other well enough to trust one another and to know how to compensate for one another in areas of weakness. Having our father as our pastor meant whatever we did in service to God through the church was a way for us to share in his ministry. Together we saw the hand of God at work. My father baptized two of his future daughters-in-law and had another one work with him as a summer missionary. He has had the privilege of coauthoring at least one book with each of his children. As we progress through this book, it will become clear just how important a heritage of faith is and how effective families working together can be in God's kingdom. But even if you are the first person in your family who follows God, your faithfulness can be an incredible blessing to your children and many generations who follow.

When Christ finished His earthly ministry and hung on the cross about to die, one of His very last acts of kindness was toward His mother.

Read John 19:26-27.

[God uses families to serve in ministry together.]

> When Jesus therefore saw His mother, and the disciple whom He loved standing by, He said to His mother, "Woman, behold your son!" Then He said to the disciple, "Behold your mother!" And from that hour that disciple took her to his own home.
> JOHN 19:26-27

4. Which of the 10 commandments did Jesus observe in this passage?

5. What does Jesus' action tell us about His relationship with John? about His responsibility toward His mother?

Although Christ appeared to deliberately distance Himself from His mother and siblings at times, He was still Mary's firstborn child, and one of His duties was to ensure His mother's care. Family mattered to Him right to the end.

Jesus' physical body was transformed into a spiritual body after the resurrection. Christ was then able to spiritually reside, or abide, in each person who surrendered to His lordship. The church, the people of God, the "called out ones," emerged as His new family and His new body, each one who did the will of His Father in heaven (Matt. 12:50).

[The Greek word used to describe the church was ekklesia or "called out ones." They were called out from the world, synagogues, idolatrous temple worship, and lives of sin and dishonest gain. They were called together by God's Spirit who replaced Christ as their leader, guide, and teacher using the apostles' eye-witness accounts of Christ and all He had taught them.]

1. Which extended family members have positively impacted you in your walk with Jesus?

2. Has anyone within your extended family not yet come to faith in Christ? How can you use your influence to share the gospel with them? (Be careful not to be pushy.)

CHURCHES BEGAN WITH FAMILIES

After Christ's resurrection and ascension, those who gathered together in His name became the church. Initially, they were not called Christians but followers of "the Way" (Acts 9:2; 19:9).

Saul was seeking to destroy the followers of "the Way" when he went to Damascus that glorious day he met Jesus. Saul was likely headed to Ananias's house to arrest the known leader among Jesus' followers. When Ananias came to return Saul's sight as Jesus commanded, the one who was blind truly saw for the first time in his life. Paul (formerly Saul) accepted God's commission to begin churches among the Gentiles (non-Jews) and spent the rest of his life encouraging and strengthening those he once sought to destroy. Paul demonstrated his compassion for families when believers in Troas gathered together in a home to hear him speak.

Read Acts 20:7-12.

On the first day of the week, we assembled to break bread. Paul spoke to them, and since he was about to depart the next day, he extended his message until midnight. There were many lamps in the room upstairs where we were assembled, and a young man named Eutychus was sitting on a window sill and sank into a deep sleep as Paul kept on speaking. When he was overcome by sleep he fell down from the third story, and was picked up dead. But Paul went down, threw himself on him, embraced him, and said, "Don't be alarmed, for his life is in him!" After going upstairs, breaking the bread, and eating, he conversed a considerable time until dawn. Then he left. They brought the boy home alive and were greatly comforted.

ACTS 20:7-12, HCSB

1. What impact do you think Eutychus's fall, death, and ultimate healing had on his family and church family?

That home was never the same again! The power of God's Word was not only spoken but it was also demonstrated for everyone in the home to see.

Families played a significant role in the apostle Paul's ministry. We don't know all the circumstances, but on at least three occasions, Paul led entire families to the Lord and baptized them. God often touches one person's heart with the intention of reaching an entire family. Once the family sees the genuine transformational difference Christ makes in a person's life they just have to find out more. Many times in the Bible and today, when one family member comes to Christ the entire family soon responds to God's love.

From Our Family to Yours

I grew up in a pastor's home, and my basement bedroom was directly below the living room. I can't begin tell you how many times I fell asleep as my father shared the living Word of God with people in need of God's power. I can certainly sympathize with Eutychus!

[We must not allow the comforts of home to keep us from God's work.]

2. Think of a time you spent in worship or prayer late at night. Describe the surroundings and what was meaningful about the gathering.

From Our Family to Yours

[**My father, Henry, tells about my grandfather starting a church.**]

"We once moved to an end-of-the-railway town that was best described as concentrated sin. My layman father was a bank branch manager and served as chairman of the Chamber of Commerce. He was involved in the community and a well-respected businessman, but his heart was to bring people to Christ. A man of integrity, Dad rented a dance hall to use as a church where he preached the gospel to the lost. He functioned by principle as a bank manager, making bank loans based more on character than on credit history. He desired to be an authentic Christian and businessman and modeled that for us kids by bringing homeless people home for the family Christmas meal.

"When we started that church, my father preached, my mother played the piano, my older brother ushered, and my younger brother and I were the congregation! I can still remember my father printing out those little titles for his message. The sign outside the dance hall said, 'Christ Crucified, Crowned and Coming,' and then listed his sermon topic. For about eight months, only our family attended, but one night a 21-year-old man stumbled in the doors we intentionally left open. So as we sang, in walked this poor guy. He seemed broken and disheartened. He sat down, and Dad preached as never before. At the invitation, my dear father said, 'Let's close our eyes.' Then I heard him say, 'If there is anybody here tonight who wants to accept Jesus Christ as your Savior, will you raise your hand?' Then I heard my father's voice cry and he said, 'Praise God, there is one who wants to be saved.' Well, we knew who that one was. That young man was saved that night. Over time, I watched God establish a church in that town that remains to this day."
—Henry Blackaby

HOUSE CHURCHES

New Testament churches had no buildings on the corners, no steeples with bells chiming the start of services, and no crosses placed outside of structures identifying them as places of worship for believers of "the Way." Most began in believers' private homes primarily for expediency and safety.

The Greek word normally reserved for families and households, *oikos*, was quickly applied to the new fledgling groups of believers who gathered together in Christ's name.

[The Greek word oikos was normally reserved for families and households but quickly applied to followers of Christ called "the Way."]

Bringing It Home
→ Ideas your family can use today ←

Child—Using the letters of your family's last name, help your child come up with words about your house, each letter representing what your house or home is like.

Teen—Send your teen a text message asking him to reply with one word that describes your home. Have a conversation with him about it later.

Adults—How would you describe the type of home you are trying to make for your family?

All Together—What do you like best about your home life? What would you change about your home life if you could?

When Saul of Tarsus began his hunt to eradicate Christians, he used a very systematic and calculated approach. Acts 8:3 says that he went house to house trying to destroy the church.

> **Saul kept trying to destroy the church. Going into one house after another, he began dragging off men and women and throwing them in prison.**
> ACTS 8:3, ISV

After Paul's conversion and missionary travels in Asia Minor, he wrote letters of encouragement and instruction to these very house churches.
• Rome: "Greet also the church in their house" (Rom. 16:5, ISV).

- Corinth: "The churches in Asia greet you. Aquila and Prisca and the church in their house greet you warmly in union with the Lord" (1 Cor. 16:19, ISV).

- Colossae: "Give my greetings to the brothers in Laodicea, especially to Nympha and the church that is in her house" (Col. 4:15, ISV).

- Colossae: "to Apphia our sister, to Archippus our fellow soldier, and to the church in your house" (Philem. 1:2, ISV).

1. Think about Saul's conversion. Name some of the ways God used him during his life and ministry. How is God still using Paul today? What allowed Paul to have such an impact?

Wealthier believers opened their homes as meeting places and guest-homes for traveling apostles, elders, or church leaders. Paul spoke to Philemon who had opened his home for church meetings.

> Prepare a guest room for me, too, for I am hoping through your prayers to be returned to you.
> PHILEMON 1:22, ISV

The fact that churches were so closely tied to homes is significant. These newly formed bodies of Christ functioned as spiritual families for new believers. They endured official persecution by the Roman government as well as unofficial harassment and persecution by the Jews who denied Christ as Messiah. Believers clung together in homes that were places of safety, warmth, and encouragement.

Bringing It Home
→ Ideas your family can use today ←

Child—Play house church. Some churches meet in homes all the time. Help your child dream. If your church met in your home, where would the preacher sit? Where would the musicians be? Do you have instruments they could use? What would you use to collect an offering? Do you have a Bible to read from? Who would lead the prayers? What snacks would you like to share after church?

Teen—Ask your teen to complete an Internet search on what a Roman house looked like and share the results with your family.

Adults—Plan a short worship service for your family with a song, a devotional, and other aspects of worship. Have your own family worship time after supper or on the weekend.

All Together—On a map of the Middle East, point out the location of the following three churches (Philippi, Corinth, and Caesarea). You may have to do a little research to find their modern names.

Roman and Corinthian houses that were big enough for a church to meet would have included a large walled, colonnaded garden or courtyard. The open areas often had fish ponds or pools that could be used for baptisms and washing and were separate from sleeping quarters and other rooms. One hundred or more people could have assembled there. These house churches could have easily surpassed the average size of most churches in the Western world today! Let's look now at three New Testament house churches.

PHILIPPI: A SELLER OF CLOTH AND A PRISON GUARD

Read Acts 16:14-15.

> A woman named Lydia, a dealer in purple cloth from the city of Thyatira, who worshiped God, was listening. The Lord opened her heart to pay attention to what was spoken by Paul. After she and her household were baptized, she urged us, "If you consider me a believer in the Lord, come and stay at my house." And she persuaded us.
> ACTS 16:14-15, HCSB

1. How did Lydia's faith in Christ affect her entire family?

Read Acts 16:30-34.

> [The jailor] brought them out and said, "Sirs, what must I do to be saved?" So they said, "Believe on the Lord Jesus Christ, and

you will be saved, you and your household." Then they spoke the word of the Lord to him and to all who were in his house. And he took them the same hour of the night and washed their stripes. And immediately he and all his family were baptized. Now when he had brought them into his house, he set food before them; and he rejoiced, having believed in God with all his household.

ACTS 16:30-34

2. Underline in the previous verses where the jailor took Paul and Silas.

No one knows all God is doing in the hearts of people. Perhaps this jailor had seen so much death that he was searching for meaning in life. Maybe he felt isolated and forgotten. Perhaps he was so racked with guilt that he wondered if his own life was worth living. He was certainly quick to unsheathe his sword to end it all (Acts 16:27)! With Paul's guidance the jailor believed in Christ and was saved. He then took his prisoners home to meet his family. Incredible! I doubt his family had either seen prisoners in their home or cleaned and bandaged their wounds. Then the family fed the apostles a meal and listened to stories about Jesus of Nazareth—how He had lived, was crucified, and was raised to life by God. Each person in the family believed that night. I imagine they had never seen their father so excited. They might have looked at their born-again father and asked, "OK, who are you, and what have you done with our real father?"

The jailor's family became pillars in the church in Philippi with Lydia's family. What a story they could tell of meeting Paul and Silas and the transformation that took place in their father's life.

1. What hard or challenging experiences have you gone through that God can use for His glory?

CORINTH: A COMMITTED COUPLE AND A SYNAGOGUE RULER

Corinth was a port city known for its wealth and the luxurious, immoral, and idolatrous lifestyle of its people. Here Paul, with Aquila and Priscilla, shared the gospel of Christ with great passion. Initially, Paul taught weekly in the local synagogue. Then after Silas and young Timothy arrived (Acts 18:5), he devoted all of his time to preaching about Christ. Crispus, the ruler of the synagogue, was convicted by his message and converted to Christ.

Crispus and his household came to Christ and were baptized together. Many other Jews and Gentiles in the city came to Christ, but the family of Crispus became central to the fledgling Corinthian church.

Read Acts 18:8.

> Now Crispus, the leader of the synagogue, believed in the Lord, along with his whole family. Many Corinthians who heard Paul also believed and were baptized.
>
> ACTS 18:8, ISV

Paul must have had families on his heart when he mentioned baptizing the family of Stephanas (1 Cor. 1:16). What is interesting about this family is their devotion to the cause of Christ and the impact they had on Paul's ministry.

Read 1 Corinthians 16:15-18.

> I urge you, brothers—for you know that the members of the family of Stephanas were the first converts in Achaia, and that they have devoted themselves to serving the saints—to submit yourselves to people like these and to anyone else who shares their labor and hard work. I am glad that Stephanas, Fortunatus, and Achaicus came here, because what was lacking they have supplied through you. They refreshed my spirit—and yours, too. Therefore, appreciate men like that.
>
> 1 CORINTHIANS 16:15-18, ISV

Paul spoke of the family of Stephanas as an integral part of church ministry as well as to his personal life. We suspect Fortunatus and Achaicus were members of his family who ministered to Paul during his incarceration in Rome. What a great example of how families can serve together. We don't have the details of how they cared for Paul, but he likely needed encouragement from the family of faith and as well as help to pay his bills while he awaited trial.

Paul also spoke of Chloe's family (1 Cor. 1:11) who visited with Paul and informed him of divisions and dissension among the church members in Corinth. Paul did not identify these family members. Regardless, Chloe's family had a vested interest in unity among the members. They were concerned enough about bickering and competition within the church that they sought outside help when they were not able to manage things on their own. This is a commendable action on behalf of a family who wants to protect their church family from the inevitable distraction, division, and destruction that accompany unresolved arguments.

Bringing It Home

→ **Ideas your family can use today** ←

[Here are a few discussion starters for your family.]

Child—What do you argue about most in your family? Are you able to work things out OK? Can you think of a time when your feelings were hurt during an argument with a brother or sister? Ask your mom and dad to help you talk about that event, and come up with a plan for how to handle it better next time.

Teen—Families have arguments, it's normal. Being able to work out differences is a great tool for getting along with others. Who is it that you argue with the most often? Why do you think this is? Make a plan to ask an older and wiser person you respect for strategies for getting along better with this person.

Adults—Churches are often similar to families, both the good and the bad parts. Do you see yourself as a peacemaker in the midst of conflict or as someone who needs to be right most of the time? Can you think of a time when you were able to help people reconcile their differences and restore their broken relationship?

All Together—Take some time to talk together as a family about conflicts in your home. You may need to ask forgiveness from one another over things that were mishandled in the past. Come up with a plan on how to handle conflict with a Christlike approach in the future.

The first churches needed to be properly established to ensure their survival and growth. Paul took great pains to help new believers understand the gospel message and appreciate their new relationship with one another. They were to treat one another with great care, just as Christ would have treated them.

CAESAREA: AN EVANGELIST AND HIS DAUGHTERS

On one of Paul's journeys, he and Luke visited Philip the Evangelist in Caesarea. Philip had been chosen as one of the first seven deacons in the early church (Acts 6:2-5). He was the first to preach to the Samaritans and demonstrated God's miraculous powers among them (Acts 8:5). The Holy Spirit led him to an encounter with a high-ranking Ethiopian eunuch he led to the Lord on the road Gaza. By the time of Paul's missionary travels, Philip had settled in Caesarea with his wife and family (Acts 21:8-9).

Read Acts 21:8-9.

> The next day we left and came to Caesarea, where we entered the house of Philip the evangelist, who was one of the Seven, and stayed with him. This man had four virgin daughters who prophesied.
>
> ACTS 21:8-9, HCSB

1. According to Acts 21:8-9, what does the fact that Philip's daughters prophesied tell you about his influence on his own family? about his family's influence on their church?

Luke, the author of Acts, noted Philip's four daughters being unmarried and having the gift of prophecy or inspired teaching. We can assume all members in their God-centered home participated in ministry and contributed to equipping God's people and sharing the gospel with the unsaved. Their church likely had an outstanding discipleship ministry with four qualified, Spirit-led women teaching Kingdom truths under the watch care of a famous evangelist dad. No wonder Paul felt welcome in their home!

It must have been fascinating for Paul to speak with Philip. The Bible records that Phillip was the first believer to take the gospel to the Gentiles as Paul was later commissioned to do. Paul would have had a wonderful time fellowshipping with Philip's family and sharing with them what he and his companions had seen in their travels.

In many cities, the family formed the bedrock of the early church. They provided a place to meet, evangelized, taught, cared for others, worked for unity, and led their families to know and serve God.

1. Compare your family to the families from the New Testament discussed in this section. What influence is your family having in your own church? in the kingdom of God?

2. One of Paul's main contributions to the early churches was to help strengthen them. How can your family help strengthen your local church? What are some ways you can help protect your church from circumstances that could potentially weaken it?

3. Name one way you can lead and protect your family so that God can use you more effectively in the church.

BALANCING HOME AND CHURCH

Read 1 Timothy 3:4-5.

"He must manage his own family well and have children who are submissive and respectful in every way. For if a man does not know how to manage his own family, how can he take care of God's church?"

1 TIMOTHY 3:4-5

The measure by which you properly lead and manage your own family will be the measure by which you are able to lead and manage those in God's family. Although the position of bishop or overseer is mentioned here, this equally applies to those who have spiritual oversight over others or who are in positions of leadership. In effect, those who give oversight to God's people need to have their own house in order before they are given places of responsibility in the church or in a ministry.

[episkopos: the Greek word for the position of bishop or overseer]

These verses have major implications. *First*, they do not say that children should have great respect for their parents because they hold the title of church deacon, elder, pastor, or teacher. Nor do they say your responsibilities at church should take priority over what is done in the home. It says that the church should respect a person and allow him to lead because of how well they first demonstrate exceptional leadership in the home.

I was absolutely thrilled when my wife and I had our first child and deeply humbled when the second and third were born. God used sleepless nights, messes, spit-up, broken figurines, and the frustration of not knowing how to console a screaming child to shape and mold my character. I grew more patient, understanding, gentle, giving, and disciplined over the years. I can handle certain things because of my deep love for my children that I might not put up with otherwise. It is true that "love covers a multitude of sins" (1 Pet. 4:8, HCSB). I look at my teenagers and know that as they have grown physically, I have grown in character, insight, and understanding. God uses these qualities as I serve Him and His people as a fellow-traveller in life.

God's people can be stubborn and difficult. They can make messes of their lives. They are like sheep that need a shepherd. Learning how to lovingly discipline our children, how to communicate with one another at home, and how to differentiate between emotional and rational responses all greatly helped prepare my wife and me for ministry.

From Our Family to Yours

Kim was away on a women's retreat, and I was in charge of my two young children for the weekend. My five-year-old son had a stubborn streak and regularly tried to assert his will over mine. Well, we had some differences of opinion that left him wishing Kim was watching him rather than me. Kim's parents lived about an hour away at the time. Their phone rang and a little voice on the other end said, "Granny, will you come and get me? Mom is gone and left me with the parent I don't like!" Raising children to be respectful and honoring to their parents has been a challenge over the years, but well worth the effort in the end.

We have served as volunteers or staff in churches for over 25 years. We have pastored, taught Bible studies, hosted home groups, led retreats, guided committees, developed ministries, and counseled many people. We have often surveyed a difficult situation then seek to guide them as a loving shepherd would guide his own flock (family).

Second, 1 Timothy 3:4-5 emphasizes that the church body must be protected. Those who seek influence without proper understanding or ability to lead God's people should not be given responsibilities over people in the church. People come into leadership for various reasons, many of which are noble. However, ulterior motives come from pride, manipulation, or the need for power, influence, or worse. Occasionally, people need to be removed from leadership because they are either ineffective or damaging. Visitors' access should be restricted when they bring with them destructive agendas. Putting incompetent leaders in charge of ministries or church activities demonstrates a lack of care and concern for those they are leading and does the whole church body a disservice.

Third, a parent's primary responsibility is to the home. God's priority is for church leaders to be spiritual leaders in the home first and out of that be better able to lead God's people. A pastor's son recently told me his father never sat down with him or his siblings to explain the plan of salvation! Although he was pretty good at sharing with others, he never took time to care for their spiritual lives. What profit is there to having a great ministry if your own children and spouse are neglected and in jeopardy of turning away from God? Our goal should be to have our priorities in the right place. If they are correctly aligned, the investment of our time and resources will follow.

From Our Family to Yours

[A solid family life can indicate the integrity and character needed for guiding God's people.]

In interviews with my last two churches, I told them my family would receive first priority in major calendar conflicts. I may serve in many churches over the years, but I have only one family to raise. The senior pastor in one church and the chairman of deacons in the other said to me, "What you said about your family commitment is a nice thought, but it isn't realistic." And I replied, "Just watch me." Over the next 13 years of ministry there, I kept that promise! I believe church leaders who demonstrate that their marriage and family come first after God can be a tremendous blessing to others. People who have not learned to distinguish "church" from God have trouble with this. Loving God with all your heart, soul, strength, and mind is not the same as being at every church-calendared event!

Without a significant investment in one's children, it will be very difficult to serve together as a family. The church cannot function properly without strong families to support it, and the family cannot accomplish all that God intends without a strong church supporting it.

Children often develop the same passions their parents possess and can easily catch the relationship parents have with God. When children watch their parents love and serve God, they will want to love and serve Him also, particularly when all are involved in ministry activities. It is easy for us to see how Abraham's faith impacted Isaac's, how Isaac's faith impacted Jacob's, how Philip's daughters followed in his footsteps, or how easy it was for Stephanus's sons join him in ministering to Paul. The relationship parents have with God should always be lived out in the home first so it can have a significant impact outside of the home. The spiritual investments we make today in our kids can reap amazing benefits in the future.

Although this verse was written concerning salvation, it's a great one to remember when parenting: "For by grace you have been saved through faith, and that not of yourselves; it is the gift of God, not of works, lest anyone should boast" (Eph. 2:8-9). We say we believe we are saved through faith, and then act like we are saved through works! Model a life of works, and you may find that faith and grace may never show up. Model for your children a life of faith and grace, and the works will come in due time.

Unlocking Your Influence

As you finish looking at truth, *consider this...*

1. How will you invest in your children this week? List your children's names and ways you will invest in each of them.

2. What are you doing as a parent to help your children develop a meaningful relationship with God?

3. As a family, list your top 6 priorities. Do your time and resource investments reflect the same order that you listed?

Chapter 3

THE CHURCH
AS GOD'S FAMILY

Young Paul became all too familiar with abandonment, divorce, drugs, and self-reliance. When Paul was five years old his father left. His mother coped by self-medicating with prescription drugs and consuming alcohol for comfort, leaving her emotionally and physically unavailable to her two young boys for days at a time. Paul sought many times to renew a relationship with his father, but each attempt was rebuffed or ignored. He and his brother tried the Big Brother association but after several Big Brothers moved on, they became disillusioned and refused to invest emotionally in those who seemed to abandon them as their father had.

Growing up in government housing is often challenging and overwhelming, but God had a plan for Paul and began working in his heart. At God's prompting Paul and his brother made their way to a local church, getting up early on Sundays to catch the bus an hour before church started. Though Paul's brother later gave up on God and the church, Paul kept going. Even though the teens at church could be merciless in their criticism of Paul's lack of biblical knowledge, he persisted in his search for God. A loving English teacher named Marg took an interest in Paul and saw potential in him when no one else seemed to care. As they talked, they realized they attended the same church. Abandoned by his father, neglected by his mother, ostracized by his youth group, and at odds with his brother, Paul found a spiritual mother who refused to abandon him. When Paul's father and mother passed away, the bond between him and this godly teacher grew deeper and more profound. Until his dying days, Paul's father ignored him, but Paul found a heavenly Father who deeply loved him and stood by him. Paul now serves on a church staff as a minister to children, and he and his wife have adopted two orphans from Africa in an effort to give to others what he never had in an earthly family. Paul's five children have a God-centered home and loving spiritual brothers and sisters at church.

> "The church, as a community of faith, is a place for believers to gather in the name of Christ, drawn together by His Spirit for worship, discipleship, and service."

God never intended His people to be orphans. When we are born again (1 Pet. 1:23; John 3:3) we come alive spiritually, are able to understand spiritual truth, and experience God's presence. The church, as a community of faith, is a place for believers to gather in the name of Christ, drawn together by His Spirit for worship, discipleship, and service. It becomes an immediate support network for believers and provides spiritual brothers and sisters with whom the new believer can fellowship and participate as a part of his or her new family.

THE FAMILY AS GOD'S PATTERN FOR THE CHURCH

For God's people to function in the church as God intended, they must relate to one another as brothers and sisters in Christ. Almost everything about God's relationship with His people was to be reflected both in the family and in the church.

From Our Family to Yours

[Families benefit from being involved in a local church body.]

Growing up as a pastor's kid, the church became the Blackaby family's second home. In the early days we arrived an hour before Sunday School to mop up the water that had seeped into the basement from a cracked floor so classes could meet without getting their feet wet. At other times we helped carry plywood and nails for the additions we built to the church. We were ushers, greeters, choir members, committee members, worship leaders, student preachers, musicians, and more over the years. Church was a place where we met our friends, found our prayer support in tough times, arranged our first dates, and began to find out how God had gifted us for His service. So many things happened in our lives through the church that there is no possible way to measure the impact our church family had on us over the years.

Now as parents we see how our own children have benefited from being a part of the church. My older son learned to play the drums at church and now plays for praise teams and in the high school band. My daughter helped in children's programs, learned how to guide children, and now is in demand as a babysitter. She also had opportunities to sing and play the piano in worship. Both learned leadership skills in the youth program and had opportunities to serve on mission teams, praise teams, summer kids clubs, and various other service venues at church. Our younger son loves church and is always the first ready on Sundays. But most of all, our kids have learned to love God's people and let them into their lives.

1. If you were raised in church, can you name some positive memories from growing up in church?

2. Ask your children what first comes to mind when they think about church.

Not everyone has experienced church as a family or found a place they feel they can use their gifts or be involved in significant ways. Sometimes churches struggle to create a sense of family among their membership, and relationships may seem impersonal. Paul needed only one person to help him feel connected to a church family. Every person can take the initiative to draw others into God's family and love others as God has loved them.

Read 1 John 4:9,11.

God has sent His only begotten Son into the world, that we might live through Him. ... Beloved, if God so loved us, we also ought to love one another.
1 JOHN 4:9,11

3. What does 1 John 4:9,11 tell you about God's love?

Read John 15:12-13.

> "My commandment is this: love one another, just as I love you.
> The greatest love a person can have for his friends is to give his
> life for them."
>
> JOHN 15:12-13, GNB

4. What do Jesus' words in John 15:12-13 tell you about what it means to be
   a true friend and about demonstrating love?

To know how to love our families and our friends, we only need to look at
how God demonstrated His love toward us. To know how to lead his family, a
father only has to look at the way God led His people. When a man wants to
know how to treat his wife, he can look at how Christ willingly gave His life
for His church.

Mothers can show Christ's sacrificial love toward their children, and
so can individuals as they care for one another in the church. Parents can
protect their children and pastors their congregations as God protected His
children as they wandered through the Sinai wilderness. Parents in the home
and leaders in the church can provide the same nurturing sustenance as God
provided His children.

5. How would you describe yourself when it comes to showing love to those
   around you?

○ I am very good at demonstrating love.
○ I am OK at demonstrating love.
○ I don't have trouble, but I don't go overboard.
○ I have trouble demonstrating love.
○ Other:_____

Families' imperfections are also common in the church. The church extends
compassion, grace, forgiveness, sacrificial love, and acts of kindness, but it
also exhibits complaining, bickering, back-stabbing, criticism, and selfish-
ness. The Holy Spirit works in Christians to help forgive, exhort, rebuke, love,
and offer grace to one another so we can all grow together in Christ.

From Our Family to Yours

"Lisa and I faced issues in the church at times, but we always tried to think through with our kids how they might be addressed. We encouraged our kids to be a part of the solution. For example, when the music director faced a lot of criticism, I agreed with some of it and talked with my boys about some of my philosophical issues. Then the boys and I took the director out for lunch to encourage him. As a result, our kids learned you don't have to like or agree with everything in your church for it to be a good church."—**Richard Blackaby**

[My brother, Richard, writes about including his family in solving difficult issues at church.]

GODLY INFLUENCE ON YOUR FAMILY

I met many of my childhood heroes through church. Some were older, seasoned Christians who had dedicated their lives to serving the Lord. Others were vibrant, excited new Christians with contagious, faith-filled outlooks. Many of the veteran Christians visited with my father in our home or sat with us at our supper table from time to time. Rather than seeing our home as a hideaway, we valued having God's people bless our home and family with their presence. Seeking people who have hearts for God and inviting them into your home and lives is valuable. They need not be missionaries, pastors, or ministers. They can be ordinary people who love God and enjoy serving Him where they are. Their stories about God's faithfulness will leave lasting impressions on your children as well as increase your faith.

From Our Family to Yours

"We often invited missionaries into our home for dinner, and our children visited with them, asked questions, and heard some amazing stories about God's work around the world. Almost any family can volunteer to host missionaries, drive them around, or have them over for meals. We also tried to surround our children with people who love God. They looked up to the mature Christians who, in turn, tremendously impacted their lives and understanding of what being a Christian means."
—**Marilynn Blackaby**

[My mother, Marilynn, writes about the importance of missionaries' influence on our family.]

1. If you could have dinner with a pastor, missionary, or a seasoned Christian, what questions would you ask?

2. Identify two or three people in your church or community who have a heart for God. Plan a time to invite them for dinner.

LOVING GOD'S PEOPLE

We as Christians should find fellowship with other believers through the church where we can serve and work together for God's glory. Regardless of the differences between us and fellow believers, we are commanded to "love one another earnestly from a pure heart" (1 Pet. 1:22, HCSB).

Read 1 Peter 4:8-10.

> Above all, continue to love each other deeply, because love covers a multitude of sins. Show hospitality to one another without complaining. As good servant managers of God's grace in its various forms, serve one another with the gift each of you has received.
>
> 1 PETER 4:8-10, ISV

Many churches lack genuine love for one another. Members may tolerate each other and work or serve together but do not actually love one another as Christ intends.

Read Philippians 2:1-4.

> Is there any encouragement from belonging to Christ? Any comfort from his love? Any fellowship together in the Spirit? Are your hearts tender and compassionate? Then make me truly happy by agreeing wholeheartedly with each other, loving one another, and working together with one mind and purpose. Don't be selfish; don't try to impress others. Be humble, thinking of others as better than yourselves. Don't look out only for your own interests, but take an interest in others, too.
>
> PHILIPPIANS 2:1-4, NLT

1. Underline in Philippians 2:1-4 how we should show love for one another.

Loving others means each person should value unity and the needs of others over personal opinions and agendas. It means having great joy in others' successes and encouraging them in their accomplishments. It involves serving others and not waiting to be served. It means taking an interest in the lives and journeys of others regardless of whether others show an interest in you.

WHEN GOD ADDS TO THE FAMILY

As Christ's church, we must consider that as He directs the lives of believers, He may in fact be sending them to various churches for significant reasons. When Christ sends people to His churches, He expects the churches to treat them as they would treat Him. Churches who take seriously their role as spiritual families have an inclusive attitude that welcomes all visitors, strangers, those who are hurting, and those who are serving as well as those looking for a spiritual home and those who want to connect with fellow believers. Every visitor should be welcomed as a brother and sister in the Lord rather than looked at with suspicion, seen as a potential threat to the status quo, or simply ignored.

> "I am telling you the truth: whoever receives anyone I send receives me also; and whoever receives me receives him who sent me."
> JOHN 13:20, GNB

Erika arrived at the international church in Norway all alone one Sunday. This English congregation quickly realized that she spoke only Spanish, was not very familiar with church, and had nowhere else to turn. Fortunately, a few people who had lived in Venezuela could communicate with her. Having left her family in Chile to look for work in Europe, she had nowhere to live, no job prospects, and could not communicate in Norwegian. The church members quickly found her a place to live with a family who spoke Spanish and began to help her learn the local dialect. Several church members hired her to clean their homes to provide her with some income. Others helped her navigate the government employment agencies and read the papers for jobs in her area of training. Over the next six months, Erika came to know the love of Christ and gave her heart to the Lord. Because she could find no work in her field, she returned to her children and husband in Chile, but she returned as a new person who had experienced a church as family both physically and spiritually.

Simply being friendly to visitors and drawing them into the heart and life of your church family are very different things.

Simply being friendly to visitors and drawing them into the heart and life of your church family are very different things. New people often bring new ideas and sometimes question why things are done a certain way. They may not always agree with the church's direction or may seem to constantly compare things with how things were done in their last church! Some people may see this as threatening, but others may view it as a very exciting time because they see each person as sent by God.

The mission statement of First Baptist Church, Biloxi, is "To grow as a Christ-centered family. We believe that a sense of community happens when people experience the change that Jesus alone can make in their lives." One of many churches who dealt with the devastation of Hurricane Katrina, more than one hundred of their families lost their homes. They learned quickly the importance of a church family that supports families. They have a loving, discipling, God-centered community of believers who are helping families serve together on mission around the world and in their own community.

Feeling like family in the church means:
- You are accepted and you feel you belong.
- The people actively take an interest in your life.
- People care for you and help you when you are in need.
- People pray for you and look out for you.
- You have a place to serve and are given responsibility.
- You have a contribution to make.
- You are included.
- You are nurtured and fed spiritually.

Unlocking Your Influence

As you finish looking at truth, *consider this...*

1. What are some practical steps you can take to better demonstrate love to those around you?

2. How would you deal with someone who comes to your church or community and does not speak English? How can you help them get acquainted with the community?

3. Describe what you think it takes for a church to feel like family to someone.

FAMILIES EXTEND THE MISSION OF THE CHURCH

Home and church ideally share the same values, purposes, and mission. Things such as respect for one another, caring for one another's needs, helping the young grow into maturity, and helping one another develop talents, gifts, and abilities should be in the home and in the church. A family who takes seriously their relationship with God and involvement with His people will begin to incorporate the mission of the church with the mission of their family. This will give a family intentionality in what they do so they will live with purpose and understanding of what it means to be servants of God.

> " A family who takes seriously their relationship with God and involvement with His people will begin to incorporate the mission of the church with the mission of their family. "

THE CHURCH SHARES THE GOOD NEWS OF CHRIST

Everything a church does should have the ultimate goal of bringing people to God. When a family accepts that the mission of the church is also the mission of their family, they will begin to look for chances to share the gospel. Going to the park with your preschooler becomes an adventure to see if God has someone there who needs a friend. Sitting in the stands at your son's basketball game turns into an opportunity to invite another parent to church. Organizing a class outing for your daughter, hosting a birthday party in your home, and inviting neighbors into your home become ways to connect with people and to see if the Lord has something in mind for you to do as "salt and light" in your community (Matt. 5:13-15).

Read Matthew 5:13-15.

"You are the salt of the earth; but if the salt loses its flavor, how shall it be seasoned? It is then good for nothing but to be thrown out and trampled underfoot by men. You are the light of the world. A city that is set on a hill cannot be hidden. Nor do they light a lamp and put it under a basket, but on a lampstand, and it gives light to all who are in the house."

MATTHEW 5:13-15

When God saves an individual, He has a whole family in mind. Our relationship with God is always meant to be shared, with our family first and everyone else after that!

1. Do you find it hard to share about Jesus with friends or family? Explain your answer.

2. How can you become more comfortable talking about Jesus with others?

One Family's Story

Connie had been running from God for many years. The church she had grown up in was heavy on guilt and light on grace, and the religious rituals she enjoyed as a child no longer appealed to her. She actually began to hate everything about church. In 1973, she headed off to college. To take a break from homework, she followed her roommates to an evangelistic crusade in downtown Saskatoon, Canada. There she encountered a Christian woman who talked with her about a personal relationship with Christ and challenged her concept of Christianity. When Connie realized for the first time that God loved her and wanted to be a part of her life, she asked Christ into her heart. She began attending a local church and felt welcomed by the people she met there. The Spirit of God brought instant transformation to many areas of her life, and Connie began to share her faith with her siblings. Soon her younger sister accepted Christ, and together they began having an impact on the others. In the coming years their youngest sister and her husband were brought to faith in Christ, and now three sisters and their husbands serve God together in the same church.

Families and churches work together to bring the good news of Christ's love and sacrifice to those who have not heard it. For many it starts in the home sharing with unsaved family members. Families who are already committed to Christ can share with other families who have not yet responded to Christ.

Bringing It Home
→ Ideas your family can use today ←

Child—Probably not all of your child's friends have heard that Jesus loves them. Some of them might come with you to your church if you invite them. Take time to help your child make some invitations for their friends to come to a special children's event or to be a part of a drama, musical, or program your church provides. Be sure to put your phone number on the invitation in case their parents have questions. Pray that some of your friends will come to know Jesus too.

Teen—Depression, anger, suicide, theft, vandalism, drugs, sex, pornography, computer addiction, and world religions are trapping many teenagers today because they do not know Jesus personally. Talk to your teen about these things. Encourage him to ask God to give him the opportunity to share Jesus with one of his friends and that he doesn't get mixed up with other destructive things. Remind him to invite a non-church friend to an upcoming church youth event. Pray together that this friend would respond positively to Christ.

Adult—Explain the basic steps of salvation to your children in terms they can understand. 1. God loves you and has a wonderful plan for your life (John 3:16); 2. Our sin broke that relationship and offended God (Rom. 6:23); 3. God sent Jesus to pay the price for our sin so we could be forgiven (John 14:6); 4. If we trust in Christ as our Lord and Savior, He will come and live in us and help us to live a life pleasing to God (John 1:12).

All Together—Spend time praying with your children for their unsaved friends. Encourage your children to invite their friends to church activities, youth events, children's programs, or Christmas and Easter productions.

[Here are a few practical ideas to help your family be intentional about sharing the good news of Jesus with friends who are not yet Christians.]

THE CHURCH WORSHIPS

One of the most important activities of the church is to worship as individual families. In our home we worship when we honor God's name by not using it in any meaningless and empty way. Outside our home, our children hear friends at school, coaches, and other adults in their lives use God's name flippantly or take God's name in vain, but inside the home it is revered.

1. How would you define worship?

2. What are some practical ways you and your family can worship God together in your home?

We worship God through family devotions and prayer. This has taken many forms at various stages in our children's lives. When they were small, devotions were Bible stories and prayer before bed. During their elementary school years, devotions happened best after supper using tools and resources designed for families. With busy teenagers, we need to schedule devotions at different times depending on the week, and topics are often drawn from issues they or their friends may be facing. At certain stages daily family devotions may not be feasible. The goal is to inspire our children to want to know God and to apply His Word however that can happen throughout the week.

    We worship God when the music in our home praises and honors the Lord. We worship Him when we teach our children to tithe from their income, giving back to God out of gratefulness for what He has given us. We also worship Him when we make regular church attendance a family priority.

From Our Family to Yours

[My mother, Marilynn, shares how our family emphasized the importance of Sunday as a day to worship God.]

"We did our best to instill in our children the routine and commitment to be in church on Sundays to worship God. We knew as a family Sunday was a day to worship God. No sleepovers on Saturday night, year-end team parties, sports games, or practices kept us from worship. As our children grew into teenagers, the fight was not whether we would go to church but what they were allowed to wear when they went!"
—Marilynn Blackaby

From Our Family to Yours

I (Kim) remember occasions when Tom was away and I got myself and three young children ready for church. Invariably, I spent the church service in the nursery or managing the children and returned home worn out, feeling that I had not worshipped at all. When I remarked to Marilynn that it didn't seem worth the effort, she reminded me that I was establishing a pattern for my children and modeling that church is important regardless of how I feel on a particular day or how much trouble it may have been to get there.

THE CHURCH SERVES

Christ commanded us to love God and our neighbor, and serving them is the best way to demonstrate our love. Have you ever made food for the family whose mother was ill? Have you ever cleaned up your neighbor's scattered trash or shovelled snow simply because you were physically able? How about watching the young children of a couple who have not gone out for an evening alone in months or years? What about helping someone move who could not afford a moving company? Have you taken groceries to an elderly person on a limited income? How about filling a shoe box of goodies and supplies to be sent overseas to needy people or making sandwiches for the homeless? Have you taken clothes to a ministry to the needy or manned a Salvation Army collection kettle? All of these things can be done as a family and demonstrate our servant hearts—things done without any expectation of remuneration, gratitude, or reward.

Sometimes we need to serve people in more substantial ways, such as caring for a family whose spouse has been incarcerated or taking in foreign students who have nowhere to go at Christmas or Thanksgiving. Sometimes service can mean walking with a single mother who is having trouble raising her children or making sure families with special needs children are included in fellowship and discipleship as much as possible. Your whole family can share in these ministries as you open your home, toys, and lives to someone in need.

Unfortunately, many people do not appreciate this aspect of Christlikeness. They live for themselves, vacations, acquiring more stuff for their homes, and bigger and better toys to fill their time with pleasure and personal gratification. Such people seem oblivious to the many people around them who daily struggle to put food on the table or to pay their mortgage to keep their home. Service shows our gratitude to God for all He has given us physically, spiritually, and socially. It demonstrates to others our love for them and God at the same time. Service is a significant part of the Christian life that is best learned at an early age.

Read Matthew 20:28.

> "The Son of Man did not come to be served, but to serve, and to give His life a ransom for many."
>
> MATTHEW 20:28

1. How do Jesus' words about His ministry impact your own thoughts about serving people?

One Family's <u>Story</u>

Dean Black is a certified mechanic who gets great joy out of helping others. He often donates his time to fix cars for people who have limited income, charging them only for the cost of parts. I've been with him many times when he received a phone call from someone desperately needing advice. When a customer at his shop decided to sell his car rather than repair it, Dean bought it from him. He fixed up the car on his own time and gave it to a church family in desperate need of a reliable car. To this family Dean is a saint and an answer to prayer.

THE CHURCH HELPS CHRISTIANS GROW

Read Matthew 28:18-20.

> Jesus came and spoke to them, saying, "All authority has been given to Me in heaven and on earth. Go therefore and make disciples of all the nations, baptizing them in the name of the Father and of the Son and of the Holy Spirit, teaching them to observe all things that I have commanded you; and lo, I am with you always, even to the end of the age."
>
> MATTHEW 28:18-20

Christ commanded us to make disciples, teaching them to follow all that He commanded (Matt. 28:18-20). Reading Bible stories to your children, posting Scripture memory verses in your home that teach your children about God, discussing the Sunday sermon with our children on the way home from church, and asking about what they learned in Sunday School, home group, or Bible study are great ways to ensure our kids grow in their faith. We also pray with our children about the coming week and assure them that God will guide them through the tough situations they face.

The church can only supplement or reinforce what the parents are already doing at home to help their children grow spiritually. Far too many parents have all but abandoned their responsibility for the spiritual growth of their children. Some parents believe that as long as they make sure their kids go to Sunday School, kid's club, or Bible study group, they have done their duty.

Rick Osborne, Christian author of more than 40 books on children and parenting says, "Current statistics show that well over 70 percent of children who are raised in the church leave the church after graduation. Why? There are a number of different factors but most agree that probably the number one reason is that most Christian kids never mature in their knowledge and experience of the Faith. If we taught our children math and science in the same haphazard way we teach them about their Faith not one of them would graduate."[1]

Many parents feel inadequate to teach their children about spiritual things. A healthy church will equip you to do that! A good place to start is to begin sharing what God is teaching you each day so your children can grow with you as you grow in the Lord. Remember, your children will learn far more from watching you than from listening to you. As you demonstrate your faith, openly pray to God, are seen studying His Word, serve others, and as you open your home for Bible studies, youth activities, and church events, they will see your devotion to God and His people. It will impact them more than you can imagine.

1. What did Jesus mean when He commanded His followers to make disciples (Matt. 28:18-20)?

2. Jesus' idea of making disciples was to teach others everything He commanded. Do you know what Christ commanded? Use this question as an opportunity for your family to help each other learn and grow spiritually.

1. Rick Osborne, "1,000,000 Christian Parents Raising Disciples for Christ," [online], [cited 26 February 2009]. Available from the Internet: www.facebook.com.

Bringing It Home

→ Ideas your family can use today ←

Child—Think of three or four adults who care about you. Do you remember how they walk and how they talk? Can you pretend to be them and say something they told you? Thank God for letting these special people be in your life.

Teen—Encourage your teen to make a list people who have been an influence in his life for the past five years, including parents, grandparents, youth leaders, pastor, teachers, coaches, and so forth. Tell him to write one or two things he has learned from them. Ask, "Who has had the most impact on your life?"

Adult—In the two columns below, list those things the church is responsible to teach your children under "church" and list the things parents are responsible to teach under "home." What do you notice?

All Together—Think together as a family how you would tell people about God's love for them without using any words at all. How could you show them God loves them (pictures, actions, gifts, help, take them to church, and so forth)?

CHURCH	HOME

THE CHURCH STRENGTHENS FAMILIES

Churches today are adept at planning youth activities and Bible studies, children's church and vacation Bible schools, women's Bible studies, and men's outreach activities. These programs are all great for discipling Christians and helping them grow spiritually but sometimes leave a very obvious void when one looks for churches that help families become stronger and more intentional in their ministry. We need to provide activities that build unity in the family and help parents talk with their teenagers. Churches should offer to help families serve together and give parents scriptural and spiritual guidelines for raising their kids in the Lord. It is hard enough as it is to get our teenagers to talk with us during the week, but sending them off on Sundays to separate buildings with separate worship, separate Bible Studies that promote separate social activities will not address this problem.

Some churches offer glimmers of hope, however. We see family camps and mother-daughter retreats. We see father-son breakfasts and family Fall Festivals. But most churches could do more to encourage families to grow together instead of planning increasingly more activities to separate them from one another. It is not difficult to have a Family Fun Night, a Family Bowling Night, a barbecue or picnic with family activities, or even Bible quiz nights for the family. We need churches that will design activities and programs to encourage families not only to grow together but to serve together! One wonders why so many churches have abandoned this responsibility in a day and age when families seem to be under attack from every angle.

North Sea Baptist Church provides a night of activities designed to allow every member of the family to participate (except babies!): balloon volleyball in the auditorium, ping-pong blow ball in the foyer, indoor soccer in the fellowship hall, relay races, and scavenger hunts around the property. Each deacon acts as a team leader and receives a portion of the church membership list from which they enlist their teams. Name tags are made, team banners are designed, and prizes are awarded at the end for the teams with the most points. Dads and daughters hit balloons together, mothers and sons try to blow the ping-pong ball across the table without losing their chewing gum, and teenagers drip with sweat as they try to score a goal on the deacon chairman guarding the soccer net—what a blast! More people come to these events than any other event hosted by the church all year! Why? Because families are desperate for something they can do together in a healthy and encouraging environment.

Many churches who can afford it have opted for building recreation centers, family activity facilities that house gyms, weight rooms, banquet halls, bowling alleys, game rooms, and more in an attempt to provide their people with meaningful family activities. But this is not possible for the vast majority of churches, so they have to be much more creative and intentional in their planning for families.

Youth pastor David Fresh plans weekend retreats for mothers and daughters to come together overnight away from the busyness of their home life. Both mothers and daughters prepare and deliver devotionals, the pastor provides a Bible study for them to work through together, and times of formal and information sharing throughout the weekend promote intimacy and communication. This provides moms with an opportunity to talk with their daughters and get to know them on a deeper, even different level. For some moms and daughters it is a highlight of the year and a chance to build lifelong memories. For others not used to sharing at such a personal level, this can at first feel threatening or uncomfortable. However, it is important to have personal discussion and communication on spiritual topics so that families can seek the Lord and grow together.

Mark Holmen describes for churches and pastors what it looks like to support families:

- Men's and women's ministries equip individuals to live their faith at home.
- Small-group ministries focus on equipping people and holding them accountable for living out their faith in their homes.
- Your prayer ministry equips every family to pray daily in their homes instead of focusing on a few big prayer events at the church.
- Sermons include an emphasis on taking the message home and living it out on a daily basis.
- Your church's Bible studies equip adults to be like Christ in their homes, community, and world.
- The children's ministry helps equip parents to talk with their children about faith.
- Your youth ministry helps parents keep their teenagers engaged in a walk with the Lord through ongoing faith talk in the home.
- Outreach ministries refocus what they do to allow families to be involved in outreach as a family.
- Preaching and teaching would provide practical examples and personal challenges for Christlike living in the home. Fill-in-the-blank sermon notes include a Take It Home section filled with questions to consider, application ideas to implement, and additional Scriptures to study.[1]

Churches that value and encourage their families will have limitless resources and opportunities for impacting their communities and their world.

One Family's Story

"I have a dream of a Christian community where children, youth, middle-aged and seniors, boomers, busters, gen-Xers and millennials learn to respect and love and discover their profound need for each other; where people from all wealth and power backgrounds can live and relate and laugh together.

"I have a dream of a family where singles and married couples, and married couples with families, and single parents, and divorcees are all affirmed in their worth before God as his people; a family where poor and rich, sophisticated and unsophisticated, the physically and mentally strong and the physically and mentally challenged have learned to walk together in love and to appreciate and affirm each other."
—Bruce Milne[2]

Bringing It Home
→ Ideas your family can use today ←

Child—Do you remember your first day of school? Were you nervous? Did you wonder if you would have any friends or if you would like your teacher? Can you think of what it would be like to go to a new church for the first time where you did not know anyone? Next week if you see a new kid your age in church, invite them to come to the children's program with you or ask if their family can sit with you in church.

[**Discuss these questions with your family.**]

Teen—Do you see any "fringe" youth only once in a while at church? Do you know their names? Do you have enough courage to ask them to sit with you or your group the next time you see them? Try to get their e-mail address or phone number and make sure they are invited to your next youth social.

Adult—Do visitors see your church as welcoming and friendly or cold and judgmental? What do you do to help new people fit into their new spiritual home? Do you visit them at their home to see if they have any questions about their new community or the church? Do you learn about their background and spiritual gifts to help them serve God where He has brought them?

1. Mark Holmen, *Building Faith at Home: Why Faith at Home Must Be Your Church's #1 Priority*, (California: Regal Books, 2007), 79-80, 93.

2. Bruce Milne, *Dynamic Diversity: Bridging Class, Age, Race, and Gender in the Church*, (Illinois: InterVarsity Press, 2007), 174.

All Together—Next Sunday invite a family you do not know well to go for lunch after church or get their number and have them over to your home for lunch next week.

THE CHURCH IS ON MISSION WITH GOD

The essence and the goal of being on mission as a family is simply sharing God's love with those around them, serving others in the name of Jesus, and being a family of influence wherever God has placed them.

Read Romans 10:13-15.

> "Everyone who calls on the name of the Lord will be saved." How, then, can people call on someone they have not believed? And how can they believe in someone they have not heard about? And how can they hear without someone preaching? And how can people preach unless they are sent? As it is written, "How beautiful are those who bring the good news!"
>
> ROMANS 10:13-15, ISV

1. What does this verse tell you about your responsibility as a Christian?

Paul was writing not to preachers and missionaries but to believers in house churches in Rome. It was up to each person to be light in a dark world. Read Matthew 5:16.

> Let your light so shine before men, that they may see your good works and glorify your Father in heaven.
>
> MATTHEW 5:16

The verses we read from Romans also mean that we should be alert to the activity of God around our families and recognizing God's invitation to become involved in what He is doing. Our family began to notice the teenagers who liked to hang out at our home. Most had little religious or church background but enjoyed being in our home and found it welcoming and inviting. They would comment on the "fancy dinners" we served. My wife marvelled that they considered meatloaf a "fancy dinner" until she realized it wasn't the menu they meant, it was the experience of a family that sat down to eat a home-cooked meal together with a table properly set!

They comment on the "strange" relationship that exists between our children because our kids actually *like* spending time with each other! They didn't see our children criticizing or arguing with each other or calling each other names. Our family was different, and it intrigued them.

Many teens today do not have adults who are available to them after school or in the evenings to talk, check up on them, or be interested in their lives. Their parents are working and busy with their own activities. They assume their teens' growing independence is good. We listen to the teens who come into our home, purposefully engage them in conversation, and seek opportunities to share the love of Christ with them. Sometimes God will bring the mission field right to your own doorstep. Other times He takes you to where the greatest need is.

" Sometimes God will bring the mission field right to your own doorstep. Other times He takes you to where the greatest need is. "

Unlocking Your Influence

As you finish looking at truth, *consider this...*

1. The best way to pursue God and His purposes is to make a plan. Together, make a list of goals and action steps for your family that will help you be on mission with God. Include times of worship, service, evangelism, and prayer.

→ <u>Chapter 4</u>

BECOMING
A FAMILY
GOD USES

Mark Holmen says, "I believe it is time for the church to rescue families. Further, I believe that this can only happen by reestablishing the home as the primary place where faith is nurtured. For the past several decades, the Church has poured time, energy, and resources into creating and implementing entertaining and educational programs. Yet these programs have done very little to equip parents to pass on faith to their children. Worse, the Church has created a drop-off mentality that has enabled parents to abdicate their faith-nurturing responsibility."[1]

Our actions speak louder than our words. What we model for our children in the home is what will often guide them throughout their lives. Our morals, values, integrity, and character all play a huge role in our children's development and can influence their marriages, family lives, and jobs. Our walks with God will either give them a great advantage in life or be a tremendous hindrance to them. While children are young, we need to explain to them why we go to church, sing songs of praise and worship, tithe our income to God, help others, and give money to mission causes. Let's dig a little deeper to see how we can better become a family that God uses.

1. Mark Holmen, *Building Faith at Home: Why Faith at Home Must Be Your Church's #1 Priority*, (California: Regal Books, 2007), 12.

GOD USES FAMILIES WHO SEEK HIM

Read Joshua 24:15.

> "Choose for yourselves this day whom you will serve, whether the gods which your fathers served that were on the other side of the River, or the gods of the Amorites, in whose land you dwell. But as for me and my house, we will serve the LORD."
>
> JOSHUA 24:15

Joshua was probably the oldest person still alive in the Israelite camp when he said this. All of his generation, except Caleb's and Moses' families, had died in the wilderness because of their sin against God. Joshua began as a slave in Egypt and later stood in the promised land as a free man. He saw many battles as he fought his way from Egypt to the Jordan River and beyond and many miracles as God provided for their needs of food and safety time and time again. He saw the results of sin and rebellion as well as the results of faithfulness and trust in God. The statement he made was not casual; it was based on a lifetime of walking with God. He stood before his people with a challenge to choose once and for all whom they would serve.

1. Joshua challenged the Israelites to decide whom they would serve. Have you and your family made the decision to serve God completely?

2. What other gods fight for your attention and devotion?
   - ○ television   ○ food   ○ work
   - ○ church activities   ○ hobbies   ○ other: _____

Joshua 24:23 records the Israelites' saying, "Far be it from us that we should forsake the LORD to serve other gods ... we also will serve the LORD for He is our God" (Josh. 24:16,18).

Now read Joshua 24:23.

> "Now therefore ... put away the foreign gods which are among you, and incline your heart to the LORD God of Israel."
>
> JOSHUA 24:23

3. Do you think the people were sincere when they said they would only serve God?

Incredibly, the people were saying they would serve only the Lord God while at the same time they still had idols sitting at home on their shelves! Their words sounded great, but their actions betrayed them. To their credit, they followed Joshua's instructions and remained faithful to God, at least as long as Joshua was alive.

We know how important it is to walk carefully around our children. We too must put away those things that are inconsistent with the Christian life and incline our heart to the Lord. We will pay a price for saying one thing in public and doing another in our homes. Children are very keen observers of our every word and action. They see hypocrisy quickly and point out inconsistencies when they occur. The way we walk leaves big footprints for our children to follow, so we need to be sure our footprints are leading in the right direction!

From Our Family to Yours

"I recall the time when I was confronted with the decision of whether or not I would follow the Lord. I can honestly say that my inspiration for choosing to follow God came from watching my father's life. Not just his spiritual life, but his humanness, weaknesses, and flaws. I remember thinking if God could use someone like my father in His kingdom, then surely He would be able to use me too. Dad always gave us the freedom to be who we were and never expected us to fit any image of what people thought we should be or act like others wanted us to act. He showed us how to be genuine, honest, and real before God and those watching us. When I doubted God or when I questioned whether or not He was real, I would look at my father and know that without question God was real in my father's life, and I could depend on that."—**Mel Blackaby**

[My brother, Mel, writes about learning from our father's devotion to God.]

Bringing It Home

→ **Ideas your family can use today** ←

[Parents, the ideas on this page follow the theme of teaching our children as Jesus taught His disciples. Adapt the topics to use as conversation starters with your children.]

Child—Find a pair of your mom or dad's shoes and try to walk around in them. One day your feet will be big enough to fit these shoes. Now try to put your shoes on your mom or dad. Their feet used to fit in shoes your size, but they grew up. Ask your mom or dad what their home life was like when they were your age.

Teen—Another word for *hypocrite* is *two-faced*—showing one face to family or God and another one to friends when you are away from home. *Hypocrite* means saying one thing at home and doing the opposite when you are away from home. Look up the Roman god Janus on the Internet or in a book. God wants us to be the same person at home as we are at school and with our friends. Ask yourself if you are the same person on Facebook, MSN, Skype, or texting as you are at home or church. How do you account for any differences?

Adult—Are your actions at home (and on your computer and TV) consistent right now with what you are trying to teach your children? Or do they see or hear things at home that force them to question your integrity, honesty, or the standards you try to have them attain?

All Together—Jesus taught His disciples as He walked. He *showed* them how to live just as much as He *told* them. Plan to go for a walk with your family, preferably in a place where you can see God's creation. Point out things along the way that relate to stories in the Bible Jesus would have told (flowers: "Lily of the Valley," rocks: "solid rock, firm foundation," sky: "Jesus' ascension," wind: "calming the storm," grass: "grass withers but the word of God lasts forever," and so forth).

From Our Family to Yours

We arranged for each of our children to take enough swimming lessons to swim confidently in case of an emergency. What I always dreaded most was negotiating the wet changing room floors with my sock-covered feet as shoes were not allowed into the pool area. It was my turn to take my son for his lessons, so after helping my 5-year-old into his swimming suit, we worked our way gingerly around the water puddles toward the shower room to the pool entrance. I noticed, much to my delight, that the left side of the showers was dry and the right side was wet from swimmers showering. What I did not notice, however, was that this newly renovated shower room did not have handles for hot and cold, rather newly installed automatic motion sensors with temperature controlled mechanisms. So as I boldly walked hugging the left wall with my young son following closely behind, I set off each sensor in rapid succession which responded with a blast of water right to my son's head. Needless to say my son became increasingly agitated with me with each successive blast of water, and I looked back in dismay realizing my poor socks were going to be completely soaked when I returned. When we went home that day, I apologized to my son for being so focused on my own socks that I nearly traumatized him. Our actions often have an immediate impact on our children following in our footsteps, but at other times the results of our behaviors will not become known for years. Nevertheless, where we go, what we say, and what we do will shape and mold our children's thoughts, actions, and words.

[Children learn constantly through the behaviors of their parents.]

1. If your kids were asked what their mom or dad believes about God, based on your actions, what do you think they would say?

2. Based on your family life, how would your children define the following?

○ prayer _____   ○ trust _____

○ faith _____   ○ giving _____

3. What does your life say about who you believe God is?

SEEKING THROUGH DEVOTION TO GOD

> " Family is where we learn what it truly means to love. "

Gaby Spicer says, "We do several things to establish God as the center of our home and to help our children understand their role in the kingdom. We use service as a tool in disciplining them and helping them understand what it means to help those around us, to give, to encourage, to bless, and to provide for those that lack. We also show our kids constantly that they are important to us and that we love them and are there to serve, encourage, bless, and provide for them. We believe that our family is our first responsibility; it is where we learn what it truly means to love."

Your children need to see you visibly spending time in God's word and in prayer. You can't expect your children to have quiet times with God or to read the Bible devotionally if they never see you doing it in the home. They need to see you growing in your faith in God, knowledge of God, practice of Christian principles, worship, and love for God. Children will carry memories of their parents with them forever, and I want my children's memories to include my devotion to my Lord.

1. What time in your day do you set aside to spend with God in prayer and Bible study?

2. What memories will your children have of you in regard to your relationship with God? Will they remember your devotion to God? Are you leaving them evidence of that relationship?

LOVE GOD'S PEOPLE

Read 1 John 4:20-21.

> If someone says, "I love God," and hates his brother, he is a liar; for he who does not love his brother whom he has seen, how can he love God whom he has not seen? And this commandment we have from Him: that he who loves God must love his brother also.
>
> 1 JOHN 4:20-21

1. What does your love for other people say about your love for God?

2. Are your relationships with God and other people similar? If so, how? If not, what needs to change?

Be careful of your criticisms about other Christians, observations of church inadequacies, and discontent with how things are done at church. All of these things leave impressions on your children who may not be able to understand that we can still love people while disagreeing with them. Too many children hear character assassinations and criticisms of church leaders at home then see their parents interacting with the same people at church as if there was nothing wrong. Helping our children have a healthy understanding of God's people and His church is very important. They need to understand that church is more than a building, a bunch of activities, and a place to meet with God; it is a place where we gather together as God's family, warts and all!

3. We don't always get along with everybody. Can you think of a time when you had an argument or disagreement with someone? How did you handle that situation? Based on 1 John 4:20-21, how might you handle that situation differently?

DESIRE TO GROW

Growth implies change: change in our attitudes, character, disciplines, and choices. Desiring to grow means we will continually place ourselves where we will be challenged spiritually such as Bible studies, home groups, and accountability groups. We must move beyond our spiritual status quo and go deeper with God. We must move beyond simple devotional thoughts and seek out the deeper truths of God's Word.

Read Hebrews 5:12-14.

> In fact, though by now you should be teachers, you still need someone to teach you the basic truths of God's word. You have become people who need milk instead of solid food. For everyone who lives on milk is still a baby and does not yet know the difference between right and wrong. But solid food is for mature people, whose minds are trained by practice to distinguish good from evil.
>
> HEBREWS 5:12-14, ISV

1. What are you doing to grow and develop your relationship with God?

From Our Family to Yours

As a young woman, I would not have described myself as an angry person. I was not prone to angry outbursts. I was not negative and contentious with others. I was quite a pleasant, loving, and agreeable person. At least that is how I saw myself. However, when I found myself at home day after day raising two small children, this loving, agreeable person became irritable, impatient, harsh, critical, prone to yelling, and, yes, even angry outbursts. I didn't like the person I saw emerging, and I realized that my perfectionism was manifesting itself in some very ungodly ways. This was not the character of Christ that I professed to be seeking.

[Kim talks about desiring to grow more Christlike by depending on God's strength and His Word.]

I began to pray about this and memorize Scriptures that spoke about the character I longed to see displayed in my life. I soon realized that in my own strength, I was not able to change significantly. I needed to depend on God and His Holy Spirit to work out of my life negative and damaging traits and work into my life the fruit of the Spirit. Over time, I began to see a change. Over and over I would repeat those verses to myself and pray when I was becoming impatient or irritable. I would still find myself yelling or speaking harshly on occasion, but those occasions became less frequent, and I apologized and prayed with my kids when they did occur. They saw that their mom was seeking God and trying to change, admitting when she had sinned and seeking forgiveness. My children are teenagers now, but I can still point to the page of "anger" verses in my journal from that time and can talk about how God changed this angry mom into the one they see today.

DEPEND ON GOD

Depending on God should be a lifestyle rather than an emergency response. Many relegate God to the spiritual realm and leave Him out of the practical aspects of daily life. God spent 40 years teaching the people of Israel to depend on Him for guidance, strength, protection, and daily provisions of food, all necessities of life. Our children need to understand just how dependent we are on God for our health, safety, livelihood, and homes. Cancer,

[If we depend on God in trying circumstances, it will teach our children to do the same.]

economic downturns, tornadoes, fires, car accidents, and war can change everything in a blink of an eye. But we know that our lives are in His hands.

Read Proverbs 3:5-6.

> Trust in the Lord with all your heart, and do not rely on your own understanding; think about Him in all your ways, and He will guide you on the right paths.
> PROVERBS 3:5-6, HCSB

1. In what areas of your life are you failing to trust God? In what areas do you find it easy to trust Him?

Our children learn to be dependent on God as they watch us depend on God and see Him provide when we pray before major decisions, seek His guidance in situations, search His word for answers, and pray before panicking when a crisis arises.

From Our Family to Yours

Some years ago our family was driving near Rimini, Italy, strangely enough in a British mini-van with an automatic transmission. In Italy, most cars have manual transmissions, and all vehicles drive on the right side of the road. It was Sunday afternoon and we were sightseeing along the coast. Suddenly dashboard warning lights came on everywhere. The brakes became difficult to press, the air-conditioning went warm, and the steering wheel was fighting against me. I surmised a major belt had broken in the engine, so I asked my family to begin praying for us to find a gas station as I fought with the car. In less than a minute a gas station appeared on our side of the road. I pulled in and backed the car into a parking spot, lifted up the engine cover, and looked as helpless as I could. Sure enough the primary belt had come off the pulleys. Service stations are closed Sundays, and I had no clue who to call in Italy for help much less what the word for "tow truck" or "mechanic" was in Italian! So again we prayed for God's help. Within two minutes the owner of the station and his daughter arrived to pick something up in the office. I chased after them and motioned to my pathetic-looking vehicle. The daughter got out a phone book, called a tow truck, and instructed him to take us to the only mechanic open that day. The mechanic looked at our car, pointed to a small wheel poking out of the engine, and said, "We have no such part in all of Italy!" Again, I breathed a short prayer of desperation to God. In the end, a part was found (literally across the street from the mechanic) and we were on the road to a family conference with no loss of time to our scheduled departure. I shared the story with those at the conference, and a tall well-dressed man responded, "Tom just about the same thing happened to my car on the way here, but I have to admit, rather than asking my family to pray, they heard some pretty foul language come out of my mouth when the car broke down. I am ashamed of what my kids learned about me from how I handled that crisis." It is my desire that my children will learn by watching who their father turns to in times of crisis.

[**What will your children learn from watching you?**]

Unlocking Your Influence

As you finish looking at truth *consider this...*

1. Tell your family about something God is teaching you or about an area where you are growing in your relationship with God. Be as honest and transparent as you can.

2. Think of a scenario in which someone might become difficult to love (because of a disagreement, personality conflict, misunderstanding, or other situation). Talk with your spouse (or family if appropriate) about ways you can handle the situation while still honoring God and showing His love.

SEEKING THROUGH SERVICE

DEMONSTRATE A SERVANT HEART

In John 5:17, Jesus said, "My Father has been working until now, and I, too, am working" (ISV). This has not changed today, except now the Father, the Son, and the Spirit are working together in the hearts of people all around us. It is our turn to say, "Our Lord has been working until now, and our family is also working." Serving Christ is hard work, but it also is a joy, a privilege, and an honor and can even be a lot of fun. Serving God as a family results in deeper relationships between our family members, between us and the Lord, and between us and those to whom we minister with God's help.

> Jesus answered them, "My Father has been working until now, and I, too, am working."
> JOHN 5:17, ISV

From Our Family to Yours

Growing up in the Blackaby household meant not having a father around very much. He taught day and evening classes at our Bible school. He had meetings and Bible studies to lead. Every Sunday afternoon and every Tuesday night he drove 90 miles north to preach at a small mission church. On many occasions during the winter months we ate half-frozen sandwiches that were waiting in the car for the trip north after the morning worship service. These hour-and-a-half drives were times we could spend with our father and times we could meet with believers who wanted to study the Word of God but had no one to teach them. After two and a half years a mission pastor was called and the twice-weekly trips stopped, but a mark had been left on my life.

[**Children learn from the sacrifices their parents make to serve God.**]

As a teenager, several of us would pile into our family station wagon and drive ourselves 40 miles to lead games and a Bible study to a group of teenagers who had no church of their own to attend. Even as high school students, sacrificing to be on mission was just what we did. Some 35 years later I found myself boarding an airplane every Tuesday morning to fly 40 minutes to lead a mission Bible study and return home late at night. This continued for well over a year until a mission pastor was called and a mission church was established. My father instilled in me a desire to help people know God more by his example than by his teaching. I realized that someone had to pay the price for a church to be established. Someone had to sacrifice time and energy and resources for people to have the Scriptures opened and taught where there was no church for them to attend. My father demonstrated his willingness to be that someone, and I saw the fruit of his labor grow into a full-fledged church that in time also started several mission churches on their own. When I was faced with an opportunity to do the same thing as a teenager and later as a pastor, it did not take me long to decide I could be that someone too.

1. How do you think serving together as a family can help your children continue to seek God and share Him with others later in life?

DEMONSTRATE AN ETERNAL FOCUS

We prepare our children not just for a life on their own but for all eternity. Knowing this helps us prioritize how we spend our time and money and plan our activities. We want to have immediate, long-term, and eternal influence on our children. Showing respect for others, having personal discipline, doing their homework, and giving their best effort in sports and other interests are important to do now. Long term, we desire to see our children being faithful to carry out responsibilities, standing firm in the midst of trials, not giving in to peer pressure, and regularly attending church. Choices that will have an eternal impact on their lives are maintaining a habit of personal devotional time with God, sharing their faith with others, investing in God's kingdom, supporting missionaries and ministries, and having a strong prayer life. To adequately equip our children to handle life situations, we have to prepare them mentally with attitudes, physically with skills, and spiritually with understanding of God and His kingdom. We cannot afford to be haphazard in our approach to raising our children, hoping everything will turn out OK.

1. Are you proactive in your approach to raising your children? What areas can you be more involved in teaching and training them?

2. What do you think it means to prepare your children for eternity? How can you better do this today?

Bringing it Home

→ **Ideas your family can use today** ←

Child—Help your child use paper, scissors, markers, colored pencils, and crayons to make service coupons for your family. These can include vacuuming, picking up the house, doing dishes, raking leaves, or whatever things would be helpful or special to your family. Help them cut the coupons apart, fold them, and put them in a hat for each person to take one. Encourage them to provide this service during the coming week.

Teen—During your ride to school, or some other time, talk to your teen about ways he can serve. Some ideas include taking on a project Dad has not had time to get to, cleaning or cooking for Mom, or playing with a younger sibling without fighting. Debrief this service activity with him later.

Adult—Parents are used to serving their family, but what about your neighbors or other families in need? Galatians 5:13 says, "through love serve one another." Jesus said He did not "come to be served, but to serve" (Mark 10:45). Some have a gift of service while some struggle serving others. Ask God to give you a servant heart that is obvious to your children and spouse.

All Together—Look for a service project that your family can do together that will encourage your church, community, or other families.

From Our Family to Yours

Some time ago, Kim and I had to curtail our high school daughter's increasing reclusiveness to her room with her laptop. We were not happy with her spending so much time away from the rest of the family. We suggested that we could unplug the wireless modem if her computer time became more important than spending time with her family. Fortunately, her protests were modified by her understanding that we valued her presence and her relationship with us and her two brothers. At school the next day she told her friends how we overreacted to her computer time! One of her friends decided to test her own parents. That evening she asked, "Mom, would you mind if every day when I come home from school that I go directly to my room and spend all evening on my computer?" Her mother replied, "No," barely looking at her. There was sadness in her eyes the next day when she told my daughter that her mom didn't care whether or not she was locked in her room all evening. My daughter appreciated that, even though her parents seemed stricter than others, they actually cared to have her around and valued her as an important part of the family.

[Our relationships with our children impact them for a lifetime, both for good and for bad. Children need to know that parents value them.]

Unlocking Your Influence

As you finish looking at truth *consider this...*

1. Discuss as a family what it means to have an eternal focus. Think of one way you can approach your daily routine (going to work, school, and so forth) with an eternal focus. Record on your calendar how you will put this idea into practice this week.

STRATEGIES FOR BEING A FAMILY GOD USES

Families face a multitude of consequences due to choices that family members have made. Smothering debt, addictions, affairs, violence in the home, deceit, gambling, workaholism, abandonment, and divorce are a few of the challenges. Do these things mean God cannot use a family affected by such issues? If the issues have not properly been dealt with, the family's priority at this time is restoration, repentance, and reconciliation rather than usefulness in God's kingdom. But as a family allows God to have His way in their hearts and situations, He will show you how to use your family and home to further His kingdom and glorify His name. A few loaves and fish placed in the Master's hand can feed thousands. Though you may face more difficulties and challenges and you may need to be more creative than other families, God is able and willing to use any type of family that seeks to serve Him.

One Family's Story

Magarey really wanted to support our church but her husband was not a believer and he refused to allow her to give any money to the church. However she had two children who were always dressed in the best-quality clothing. She knew our family had four boys, all of whom were younger than her son. God told her that she could minister to the pastor's family by giving her son's slightly worn clothing to them a few items at a time. Every couple of months we would receive a box of clothes that her son had "outgrown" and each of us boys would scramble to find the best shirts, socks, or blue jeans. Our mother had to buy few clothes for her four sons while we remained in that church. She also was a great cook and always brought lots of baked goods to church events to share with others. She found ways to encourage her church family while honoring her husband's wishes. Regardless of the circumstances in which your family has come together, when you honor God in your home, it can be a powerful instrument in His hands to impact your community.

[In God's hands, a divided family, single parents, and even rebellious children have hope.]

Bringing it Home
→ Ideas your family can use today ←

Child—Sometimes parents do things that are hurtful, disappointing, or embarrassing to their children. But God is not like that, ever. Even when parents fail, God never fails. Draw a picture, or write a letter or a song to God telling Him how thankful you are that He is your God and that He loves you so very much.

Teen—Half of teens today have experienced divorce in their home. Sometimes it came as a shock, other times parents have been fighting for a long time. Being a Christian does not prevent pain, grief, or trauma; it simply grants God access to your heart, mind, and soul to walk with you through such times and give you hope that there is joy and peace ahead. The older you get, the more human and flawed your parents will seem. Take a moment now to thank God for your parent(s) and pray God will give them the wisdom and strength to parent you wisely and to depend on God when they are struggling in any way.

Adult—Every family faces struggles. The key is to turn to God together for help early in the process rather than as a last desperate act. Your children will be more confident if you are also confident in God. Can you share some struggles with your children and ask them to pray with you over them? Not to air "dirty laundry" but to genuinely bring your concerns before the Lord. Be sure to let them know what God is doing in answer to your prayer in the days ahead.

All Together—If there are wounds or brokenness in your family, be honest about them, but also look to see how God is bringing healing or other good things to compensate. Have a "funniest joke" contest where your family members find a great joke to share with others on an appointed day. Laughing together can put things in perspective and bring joy in the midst of hardship. It shows God's people can rise above difficulty and trust Him to work things out.

[Parents, help your children think of unique ways they can express their thankfulness to God. Here are some discussion-starter ideas. Teens may need to process with you the difficulties they see friends facing in their families. Be ready with a tender heart and a listening ear.]

Most single parents I know didn't plan to be single parents. Whether it was a teenage pregnancy, divorce, separation, death of a spouse, or issues of safety, they find themselves trying to be both mom and dad to their children. Single parents must be braver and stronger than others as they carry the whole load of parenting on their own shoulders, but God notices. And God will help.

Rick's wife left him, leaving him to raise three young children on his own. He wanted to honor God in the midst of his pain and rejection and determined not to add to his children's pain by slandering his wife in front of them. He worked hard, kept his kids in Christian schools, and maintained his devotion to God and positive relationships with supportive friends. His wife eventually requested a divorce and forced the sale of the family's home. Though Rick traveled a lonely road and had many questions for God, he stayed faithful and walked with integrity before his kids and others who watched him. Many years later, God brought a godly woman into Rick's life, one who also had a heart for the Lord and a heart to serve with her new husband. Together they have a wonderful ministry to parents and to families, and God has kept each of Rick's children walking with Him on the right paths. God rewards faithfulness, and God honors integrity. Rick's life is not easy, but it is blessed. God continues to use him as an encouragement to others and a witness to God's faithfulness and goodness in the midst of trials and testing.

Many families have only one Christian parent, which poses challenges to families serving the Lord. While the non-believing parent may not be overtly antagonistic to religion, the home is still divided in focus, direction, and values.

Acts 16 describes a new convert named Timothy who came from a mixed marriage: his father was a Greek (Gentile) and his mother and grandmother were Jews (Acts 16:1). Apparently only his mother and grandmother were believers in Christ. A home divided by culture and religion still produced a co-worker with the apostle Paul (Acts 17:14) and a young pastor for the early churches described in Acts and Paul's Epistles (1 Thess. 3:2; Phil. 2:19-23). Timothy was a committed believer and servant of God despite his father's likely disapproval of both his religious beliefs and life direction.

[God can choose to work through those of us who come from challenging homes.]

We are never told that Timothy's dad ever came to Christ or ever accepted his son's devotion to God, but we do know God chose to use a young man who came from a challenging home life. Paul wrote to Timothy describing his heritage of faith and encouraging him to stay strong in his commitment to Christ.

Read 2 Timothy 1:1-5.

Paul, an apostle of Christ Jesus by the will of God, according to the promise of life in Christ Jesus, to Timothy, my beloved son … I constantly remember you in my prayers night and day, longing to see you, even as I recall your tears, so that I may be filled with joy. For I am mindful of the sincere faith within you, which first dwelt in your grandmother Lois and your mother Eunice, and I am sure that it is in you as well.

2 TIMOTHY 1:1-5

One Family's Story

Friends of ours determined to be a family God could use. Although Joan and Mike were active supporters of church, their son chose to rebel against God and his family as a teenager. He moved out of the house and in with his girlfriend, breaking his parents' hearts. Joan and Mike determined to love their son and show grace despite his life choices. After much prayer they offered their basement suite for him and his girlfriend to live in, despite raised eyebrows of their church friends. Eventually their son married his girlfriend and they had a beautiful daughter. Even though their son continued to reject the Lord, Mike and Joan showed love and acceptance of their new daughter-in-law and precious granddaughter. Before long, their son and his family began occasionally attending worship services and showing up at other church events. In pursuing a loving relationship with him instead of criticizing or shunning their son and by living an authentic relationship with God before him, Mike and Joan were able to see their prodigal begin the long walk back home.

God can bring hearts that are cold toward one another and breathe new life into them, drawing them back to one another. It starts with having a clean heart toward God yourself. When your heart is turned back to God you will find your heart will also turn back to your family. When you are filled with the Spirit of God, you will be at peace with your brother and sister, spouse, or child. One of the results of people turning back to God fully is that God begins to work in their relationships with others also. Hearts that were once turned in different directions can now be aligned through God's Spirit, and they can begin to work together. Family members who were once distracted by worldly pursuits, selfish gain, personal gratification, self-centered ambitions, and indifference can now be united together through the Lord working in their hearts. If your family is divided and their hearts are not turned toward God or toward one another, ask God's Spirit to perform a miracle in their hearts and minds so that together you can serve the Lord as He intends.

PRAYER

The greatest and most effective tool parents have in their parenting tool kit is without any doubt prayer. Prayer brings the "third parent," the Spirit of God, into action.

[Make a list here of ways to pray for your children this week. Include current situations and long-term ones such as education and their future spouses.]

- Where we are not able to be with our teenagers at all times, the Lord is beside them.
- We cannot change the hearts and minds of our children, but God can.
- Although we fail and let our children down, the Lord never does.
- God brings wisdom to every difficult situation.
- He reveals the truth of every murky circumstance.
- God can unite us together as families and help us serve in His strength.
- He watches over us in our homes while we sleep.
- He takes care of our needs when we do not know where else to turn.
- He is dependable when everyone else fails us.

God as the third parent guides us through often challenging and troubled waters and raging storms and helps navigate our family safely into the harbors. Prayer can change hearts and restore relationships, brings the wayward child home and the wandering parent back, and heals the broken hearts, all things that only God can do.

VALUE EACH INDIVIDUAL

The following verses can help parents see that each member of their family is equipped in particular ways by Christ Himself to serve Him. Spiritual gifts are designed to be used for ministering to others.

Read Ephesians 4:11-14.

> He personally gave some to be apostles, some prophets, some evangelists, some pastors and teachers, for the training of the saints in the work of ministry, to build up the body of Christ, until we all reach unity in the faith and in the knowledge of God's Son, growing into a mature man with a stature measured by Christ's fullness. Then we will no longer be little children, tossed by the waves and blown around by every wind of teaching, by human cunning with cleverness in the techniques of deceit.
>
> EPHESIANS 4:11-14, HCSB

1. What do these verses tell you about God's design for your family?

Ephesians 4:12 indicates Christ gives spiritual gifts "for the training of the saints in the work of ministry, to build up the body of Christ" (HCSB). I am not suggesting children serve as pastors, go on missions as evangelists, or pray with the dying in the hospital, but they can share Bible stories with others and the basic truths of how to become a Christian and pray for those in need! They can encourage, serve, pray, sing, help, and do many things appropriate to their age in service to their Lord. They are part of Christ's body and the church, and they will have a desire to help others and serve their Lord because of the influence of Christ in your home.

Now read Peter's words in Acts 2:17.

> "This is what I will do in the last days, God says: I will pour out my Spirit on everyone. Your sons and daughters will proclaim my message; your young men will see visions, and your old men will have dreams."
>
> ACTS 2:17, GNB

2. What does this verse mean for Christians today? What does it mean specifically for you?

Peter preached these words in Jerusalem at Pentecost. This verse suggests that no one is exempt—young and old, male or female—from living out and proclaiming the message of the gospel. Moreover, this verse should sensitize parents to the fact that God may be at work in the life of one or more of your children, calling them to special service for Him. It is so exciting to see the hand of God upon your children, molding and shaping them and drawing them to know Him.

IDENTIFYING FAMILY SPIRITUAL MARKERS

An exercise in Henry Blackaby's *Experiencing God: Knowing and Doing the Will of God* is to look at the spiritual markers in your life to help determine what God's will is for the days ahead. Spiritual markers identify times of transition, decision, or direction when you clearly knew God was guiding you. These points may not come often, but they are deeply significant in your walk with God. Families can do this exercise together and write in a journal what God has done in their lives up to this point, including your tough and good times, trials and victories, and challenges and successes together. When we can identify what God has done in our past, we can better understand what

God may be up to in the days ahead. Every struggle, victory, challenge, and success, when lined up and seen in context, can give you a better picture of where God is leading your family in ministry and community involvement.

From Our Family to Yours

"The church in Saskatoon was so discouraged they decided to disband if I declined to come as pastor. When I arrived, the deacon chairman actually left because he had wanted to disband. That left us with about 10 people, and things were very hard. We worked our hearts out visiting, witnessing, and having mission groups to help us out. After three and a half years, we had 30 people in Sunday School. My oldest son said, 'Mom, I feel so sorry for dad. He preaches his heart out every Sunday, stands down at the front, and gives an invitation week after week and nobody comes.' Marilynn shared Richard's concerns with me, so I told him, 'Son, don't ever feel sorry for me. The greatest honor ever bestowed on any person is to be asked to represent God. It's more than I deserve and more than I am capable of handling. Scripture says, "He that goeth forth weeping bearing precious seed will without a shadow of doubt come again rejoicing bringing his sheaves with him."' I said, 'I don't know how long God's going to let us labor, but we believe we're where we ought to be. Son, I'm going to pray that God will let you see the harvest.' Oh, and God did! A year later the Spirit of God fell on the city and from there we began to start mission churches and see many college kids called into the ministry. And that had a deep impact on our children."—**Henry Blackaby**

Unlocking Your Influence

As you finish looking at truth *consider this...*

1. Take a few moments with each of your children from time to time and ask them what God is doing in their hearts. Ask them whether God is leading them in any particular direction or impressing certain things on their hearts. This can be a great opportunity to clarify with your children what God may be saying to them, and it will help you know better how to pray for them in the days ahead.

2. Reflect with each other about specific spiritual markers in your lives. It could be a time where God spoke to you in prayer, called you to do something challenging, or revealed Himself in a life-changing way through Scripture. Share those times as a reminder of God's grace and faithfulness.

3. Spend some time praying specifically for each other.

Chapter 5

GOD USES
CHILDREN

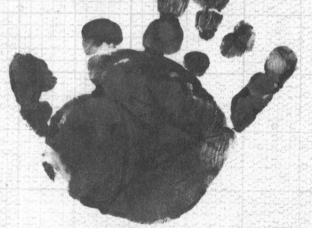

Many times as adults, we think that God can only use people who have reached a certain age. It has been said in many churches that "the youth are the future of the church." However, it is more appropriate to say that children are just as much a part of the church in the present as they will be when they become adults. Throughout Scripture, God affirms the value of children as it relates to His work, using children and teenagers often to accomplish great tasks. As our children grow, we need to constantly encourage and help them become aware of God's work in and around them. As they continue to gain understanding and experience, their influence for His kingdom will grow exponentially. In this chapter, we will discuss the role of children in God's work and examine how to prepare our children to follow God throughout their lives.

COME AS A CHILD

Read Mark 10:13-16.

Then they brought little children to Him, that He might touch them; but the disciples rebuked those who brought them. But when Jesus saw it, He was greatly displeased and said to them, "Let the little children come to Me, and do not forbid them; for of such is the kingdom of God. Assuredly, I say to you, whoever does not receive the kingdom of God as a little child will by no means enter it." And He took them up in His arms, laid His hands on them, and blessed them.

MARK 10:13-16

1. What does this passage tell you about God's heart for children?

2. What do these verses tell adults about how they should approach God?

God includes every passage in the Bible for a reason. During Christ's ministry, rich people, religious leaders, the poor, the crippled, the blind, women caught in adultery, women with broken marriages, businessmen, rulers, soldiers, and more came before Him. But in this passage, Christ saw children and infants and blessed them. As He picked up and blessed each child, I wonder if He saw into the future of what each would become and how God would use them. This was a teachable moment for His disciples and for us as Christ taught about the kingdom of God.

SOME OBSERVATIONS ABOUT CHILDREN

For the most part, children's lives are not complicated, stress-filled, corporate-driven, or laden with debt and obligations. With children, what you see is usually what you get. What they say is normally what they mean, and their emotions are easily displayed and understandable.

A child's entire world is one that is based on unconditional love, security, and trust—basic concepts common to children in every country and culture. As long as they have food, clothing, a safe place to sleep, and are loved, they are usually quite content. It is when love is withheld, safety is compromised, or the basic necessities are inadequate that emotional and physical problems begin to develop.

Children can accept things by faith that adults struggle with. If you listen to the prayers of children, you realize they have no trouble believing and trusting that God will take care of them and provide for their family's needs. Children typically have a more positive outlook on life and the future because they have no reason to doubt everything will work out for the best.

Children more likely see things as black and white rather than in shades of gray. How often have you heard your children cry, *but that's not fair?* They like justice even if it is not always possible.

If Christ says it is impossible to enter the kingdom of Heaven unless one comes as a child, then children have something to teach us about God and His expectations.

> " Children can accept things by faith that adults struggle with. "

1. How do these characteristics validate what Jesus said about receiving the kingdom in Mark 10:15?

2. Look back at the previous paragraphs. In what areas of your life could you benefit from being more childlike?

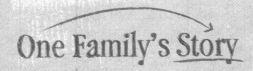

One Family's Story

"I think I knew God was calling me into the ministry as a child, but I didn't want to submit to that. I wanted to be an active Christian, but I did not want to work full-time in ministry and not get to be in the business world. I later went to my youth pastor after a youth group meeting and he prayed with me, along with some of the older youth, and I decided that God was calling me into the ministry. I went home and told my mother, and she told me that God had told her that I was going to be called into the ministry when she was still pregnant with me, but she had never told me because she did not want to influence me. This was a nice confirmation. She actually said she did not want me to be in the ministry when she was pregnant or even when I told her because she knew that ministers can have a very hard life, but she did want me to follow God."—**David Fresch**

Bringing It Home
→ Ideas your family can use today ←

[**Use these questions as a discussion guide with your family.**]

Child—How many different children can you name in the Bible? Can you remember how God used children or teenagers in the Bible? (Think about David and Goliath, Daniel in captivity, Shadrach, Meshach, and Abednego in the furnace, the boy with two fish and five loaves of bread, Samuel at the temple, and so forth.) How do you think God can use you at school or with your friends and family? If you were a missionary, where would you like God to send you? Why?

Teen—If you designed the ideal ministry organization for you to serve God, what would you call it? What would your responsibilities be in this ministry? What would your ministry goals be? How would you know if it was successful?

Adult—Has God ever given you any impressions as to what He might have in mind to do with your children? Have you ever asked Him? Write your children's names in the back of your Bible. As you study God's Word, place Scripture passages beside the names of your children that you want to pray into their lives or share with them one day when the time is right.

All Together—If children or teenagers ran the church, what changes would they make in the worship service? ministries the church offers? focus and direction of the church? church name? How do you think your church could improve on discipling, training, and loving children and teenagers? Share your ideas with a staff member at your church.

As you finish looking at truth, *consider this...*

1. Talk about some of your most vivid and enjoyable childhood memories. How have you changed since then? Which changes are good? Which changes are not?

[Talk with your spouse about these memories. Understanding changes in his or her life will help you make life decisions together.]

2. Play a game together as a family (a board game, tag, or hide-and-go-seek). Allow yourself to play like a child. Be silly and let go of any worries, stress, thoughts of work, or other responsibilities for just a little while.

VALUING CHILDREN

Another incident in the Bible describes Jesus deliberately drawing attention to a child in order to teach a valuable lesson to His disciples.

Read Mark 9:35-37.

> And He sat down, called the twelve, and said to them, "If anyone desires to be first, he shall be last of all and servant of all." Then He took a little child and set him in the midst of them. And when He had taken him in His arms, He said to them, "Whoever receives one of these little children in My name receives Me; and whoever receives Me, receives not Me but Him who sent Me."
>
> MARK 9:35-37

1. In your own words, rephrase the lesson Jesus taught His disciples.

Jesus had traveled to Capernaum where Peter's house was located. The Bible indicates He took a small child into His lap in a loving embrace. The disciples may have chuckled—that is, until the rebuke came. As they had walked to Peter's house, they argued about who would be the greatest in Christ's kingdom. When Christ asked them what they had been discussing so heatedly, they hung their heads in shame without reply (Mark 9:34). The enacted parable, part rebuke and part teaching, made quite an impact on them. Every time they saw this child they were reminded again of Christ's lesson on humility.

2. What does it mean to be humble? How does this characteristic fit into your relationships with God and with your children and family?

There was a second lesson to learn. Christ spoke in terms of a legal representative or an ambassador when He said, "Whoever receives one of these little children in My name receives Me" (Mark 9:37). Christ wants us to value children as He values them. As we treat children with love, care, respect and dignity, we do it in the name and in the place of Christ Himself. Christ wants us to love every child God puts in our family or walks through our door, every teenager who flops on our couch or grazes on our food just as He loves them. Why? Because "such is the kingdom of God" (Mark 10:14).

Would we publicly embarrass Jesus in front of His friends? No. Would we belittle, mock, or threaten Him? I hope not. Would we neglect, beat, slap, manipulate Him, or reduce Him to tears for a tiny infraction? Heaven forbid. But that is how many children are treated today. No, we would love, care for, praise, respect, and honor Him, so we should do the same for those He sends to us. This, of course, does not discount our parental responsibility disciple, rebuke, exhort, teach, and guide our children. But wait, there's more!

Read Mark 9:42.

> "If anyone causes one of these little ones who believe in me to sin, it would be better for him if a large millstone were hung around his neck and he were thrown into the sea."
> MARK 9:42, ISV

The language in the verse Mark added is strong, but the point is clear. Leading others into sin, particularly young believers, to the point where their faith is shipwrecked or shattered, is a heinous crime in the eyes of the Lord. Christ intimates that it would be better for a person to be destroyed before they were given a chance destroy the faith of others. Faith is a precious thing. To deliberately or indirectly cause another believer to sin or to turn from faith in Christ brings eternal consequences.

This passage is not necessarily speaking of children specifically, but Christ chooses to use children to teach spiritual truths about the kingdom of God. To use a child to teach adults a spiritual truth was not only creative but elevated children to a whole new level in the minds of His followers.

Bringing It Home
→ Ideas your family can use today ←

Child—Tell your children, "Sometimes parents or other adults disappoint their children. You can feel angry or sad when they let you down or fail to do what they said they would do." Ask them if there is anything you promised do to for them and have not done. If there is something, ask for their forgiveness. Read Deuteronomy 31:6 in your Bible. Then help your children make a list of 10 promises from God. Remember to emphasize that if God promised something, He will do it without fail.

Teen—Find time this week to talk with your teen about his role in the kingdom. Explain that God has something planned for him that no one else can fulfill. For help, see Ephesians 2:10 and Jeremiah 1:5.

Adult—Read Galatians 5:22-23. Which fruit of the Spirit do you feel best represents Christ to those around you? Displaying that character of Christ demonstrates that Christ lives in you. On a scale of 1-5 (1 being lowest) how are you doing with demonstrating each "fruit"?

All Together—If you have passports, take them out and let your family look through them. Notice the stamps in them (if any). Ask your children if they feel they represented their home country well when they were in another country. We may not have official ambassador status from our home country, but we represent our country to others when we encounter people in foreign countries. Ask how well each member is representing the kingdom of God at school, work, or in the community.

[Interact with your children this week. Whether or not you have passports, you can apply how you represent your family, your country, or God to vacations, in-country trips, and what you imagine you would do overseas as well.]

One Family's Story

"Going on mission trips means a lot to me. It helps us learn the meaning of life which is spreading the word of God and that some people aren't as fortunate as us."—**Lindsay Gross**, age 9

"My husband, daughter, and I decided to take a one-time mission trip to Canada. We went to a First Nation's reserve and led a kid's club for the native children. The men did construction, and the children and I led music, crafts, and drama. When the next summer came around my daughter asked—not *if* but *where* would we go on another mission trip. The next trip was to a reservation with our two little girls. The native children were fascinated with Anna, and it helped us break the ice with them. I overheard 5-year-old Lindsay telling a Native American boy that all he needed in life to be happy was Jesus. Our third trip was with our three children to South Dakota. I served in the kitchen and kept one eye on the new baby. My husband threatened that if we added a child each year we go on a trip, he would not let me come any more. That year we were blessed by our oldest daughter Lindsay accepting Christ. Tennessee and Oklahoma were our next two trips (but no more children!). When our 3- and 4-year-old kids play pretend at home, they pack a suitcase, get in their plastic Dora car, and go on a mission trip. The kids really enjoy being servants on these trips. Serving on these trips reminds us that telling others about Jesus is not reserved for the super-human career missionary. God has called us each to tell others about Jesus, both on the mission field and at home."
—**Kim Gross**

"Our family mission trips have allowed us to remain focused on what is important in life—God's love, family, and serving others. In our day-to-day lives, it is easy to lose focus on those three things and get caught up in work, school events, social activities, finances, and so forth. Giving a week each summer has given us an anchor point. A time in the near past and the near future where all that matters is God's love, family, and serving others."
—**Gary Gross**

Unlocking Your Influence

As you finish looking at truth *consider this*...

1. Discuss a time when you found it hard to be a good parent or an obedient child. What did you learn from that situation? How can you handle situations like this better in the future?

2. Examine your life for a moment. Is there anything, intentional or unintentional, that would keep someone in your sphere of influence from having a relationship with Jesus? How are you helping people see Jesus better through your life?

[Spend some time with your spouse this week to seriously consider how your family can help people see Jesus better through your lives.]

GOD'S PLANS FOR CHILDREN

Children have played a significant role in God's plans throughout history. Whenever God had in mind to do something in history to impact mankind, a child was born who God intended to use in a mighty way years later.

God intended to free His people from Egyptian slavery, so a baby was born 80 years earlier and placed in a small ark in the Nile River by his parents in order to save his life.

God wanted to demonstrate His vast love for the world, so He determined to create a nation through which He could reveal Himself to the world. A child, Isaac, was born to an elderly couple who in turn had a son named Jacob who grew to father twelve sons from which the twelve tribes of Israel descended. This family formed a lineage that led to the family of God's own Son (Gen. 29-30).

Before John the Baptist came saying, "Repent, for the kingdom of heaven is at hand" (Matt. 3:1) he was born into a family. God intended to call him into service for the King of kings and the Lord of lords to prepare the hearts of His people for the Messiah. And Gideon was born and raised by his family before God called him to lead the Israelites against the Midianite forces (Judg. 6).

It is sometimes difficult to look at your toddler, child, or teenager and see a great leader or influential person God wants to use mightily in His kingdom. But a home just like yours is where such leaders and people of influence come from. Some of those traits that greatly annoy you and test your patience today may be the very traits that will cause them to stand firm and navigate various trials later in life. Helping your children come to the knowledge of God early in their lives will give them a great advantage later on.

God's grace sees the potential of what each child can become. We see a baby, God sees a king. We see a toddler, God sees a missionary. We see a teenager, God sees a Christian CEO of an international corporation with worldwide influence.

We have no idea what God has in mind to do with our children. We just have to raise them with the anticipation that God will call them in some way to serve Him. Our primary responsibility is to prepare them so when God calls them according to His plans for their lives, they will be ready.

1. How can you better see your children as God sees them? Be specific. What areas of potential do you already see in your children?

2. What does your child do that might be frustrating now, but if cultivated properly, could be used for God's glory later in life?

Let's look at some biblical examples of children that God used for His glory.

MOSES: WHEN GOD SPARES A CHILD, IT'S FOR A REASON (EX. 2)

Jochebed defied the decrees of the king and rather than handing her infant son Moses over to be killed, she hid him from the authorities. In doing so, she put the lives of her entire family in jeopardy. She had no idea that her God-inspired act of defiance and courage would save the life of arguably the greatest leader God's people would ever know. Moses' older sister Miriam protected him as an infant and served with him as an adult (Ex. 15:20). His older brother Aaron became the first high priest before God on behalf of the nation of Israel. The Scriptures are silent on Moses' parents after his relocation to the Egyptian palace. The hardship slaves endured meant they generally did not live very long lives. When God was ready to reveal Himself to His people, Moses was the only descendant of Israel who could have voluntarily left Egypt to find God in the wilderness. All the others were confined with chains and taskmasters. A baby placed in an ark of reeds and pitch one day saw the building of the Ark of the Covenant, crafted of gold and acacia wood by the hands of free Jews. His own two sons, Gershom and Eliezer, followed after their father and continued in the priestly tribe of Levi in service to the Lord (1 Chron. 23:14).

JOSEPH: NEVER DISCOUNT THE DREAMS OF CHILDREN (GEN. 37)

At 17 years old, Joseph tended flocks with his brothers. God began to work in his life, giving him dreams of what was to come though he was not yet able to understand. He found little support from his family who mocked and ridiculed him, "Look, this dreamer is coming!" (Gen. 37:19) and who, for the most part, despised this impertinent lad. But God had plans for him. Joseph grew up in a home that could easily be called dysfunctional. His father Jacob had multiple wives who vied for his attention and whose sons were desperately jealous of Joseph and Benjamin, the sons of Rachel, Jacob's favorite wife (Gen. 37:4). The fact that she died in childbirth made these two boys even more special. Jacob unwisely used Joseph to spy on his brothers and showered him with gifts he seemingly neglected his other sons. Had Joseph's family actually listened to what the boy was saying and not been jealous or insulted by his dreams, they could have been willing participants in the wonderful plans of God. Instead they were unwitting players in a drama that God alone crafted. As Joseph later said to his brothers who sold him into slavery, "You meant evil against me; but God meant it for good, in order to bring it about as it is this day, to save many people alive" (Gen. 50:20). The son of Jacob whom everyone discounted and dismissed became the wisest man in the land and second in command over all of Egypt (Gen. 41:40). I wonder how many parents discount the dreams, insights, and heart's desires of their children instead of inquiring of the Lord as to what it may mean. I wonder how many brothers and sisters would treat their siblings differently if they knew what the Lord had in mind to do with them.

[What are your dreams? your spouse's? your children's? When you know what they are, you can ask the Lord to show you their meaning and how to make them come true for His glory.]

> "You meant evil against me; but God meant it for good, in order to bring it about as it is this day, to save many people alive."
> GENESIS 50:20

SAMUEL: TRUSTING GOD WITH OUR CHILDREN (1 SAM. 1)

Hannah vowed to God that if He would give her a child she would give him back to serve in God's temple (1 Sam. 1–2). God honored her request, and she was faithful to her vow and brought Samuel to the prophet Eli after he was old enough to enter the Lord's service (2:11). We don't know what went through her heart when that day arrived. It must have been a very difficult decision for her. I am sure many people would have counseled her against it, but God honored her devotion and chose Samuel to have a tremendous impact on His people for generations.

Each year, Hannah faithfully brought a new set of clothes and visited with her son at the temple. As time went by, she brought his three younger brothers and two sisters (1 Sam. 2:21) with her to meet him. The Bible tells us that Samuel, even as a young child, ministered before the Lord and continued to grow and serve in the temple (2:18). Scripture says Samuel "grew in stature, and in favor both with the LORD and men" (2:26). God spoke with Samuel as a boy (1 Sam. 3) and gave him important prophecies and understandings for the people to hear. "And all Israel from Dan to Beersheba knew that Samuel had been established as a prophet of the LORD" (3:20). It was rare in those days to hear a word from the Lord and even rarer to hear prophetic messages coming from a child, but God had decided it was time to raise up a new leader—one He could trust to faithfully lead His people and do all that He commanded. God said, "I will raise up for Myself a faithful priest who shall do according to what is in My heart and in My mind," (2:35).

Giving our children to the Lord is no easy thing. Trusting them and their futures completely into His hands can cause fear and anxiety for some parents. However, letting them go into God's hands is much more secure than keeping them under our watchful eye. I can only imagine how proud Hannah was to know that God was using her son as His prophet to guide and protect His people and eventually anoint Israel's first two kings.

> **"** Letting our children go into God's hands is much more secure than keeping them under our watchful eye. **"**

> All Israel from Dan to Beersheba knew that Samuel had been established as a prophet of the LORD.
>
> 1 SAMUEL 3:20

DAVID: GOD SHAPES HIS SERVANTS FROM A YOUNG AGE (1 SAM. 16)

David, the youngest of eight sons of Jesse, began as a shepherd boy tending his father's sheep near Bethlehem (1 Sam. 16:11). He guided them to graze in green pastures and beside still waters and protected them from predators. We learn that even at a young age he had the strength and fortitude to single-handedly defeat both a bear and a lion with only his shepherd's staff and a sling (1 Sam. 17:34-35). This teenager displayed not only great courage beyond his years in defeating the seasoned warrior and giant Goliath (1 Sam. 17), he also demonstrated an uncanny dependency upon God for protection and strength. His relationship with God carried him through many battles as a soldier and later provided the wisdom he needed to lead the Israelites as their king.

The greatest description of David comes from the prophet Samuel who declared to King Saul, "Now your kingdom shall not continue. The LORD has sought for Himself a man after His own heart, and the LORD has commanded him to be commander over His people, because you have not kept what the LORD commanded you" (1 Sam. 13:14). To be known as a man after God's heart is a tremendous affirmation of David's dedication and devotion to God. No other person in the Bible is given this description. Throughout David's life he faced many challenges including attempted assassination, concerted efforts to overthrow his rule, adultery, murder, and great disappointment in not being able to build a temple for God's dwelling place. Nevertheless, David maintained the same devotion to God in maturity as he had in his youth. The young boy who tended the sheep for his earthly father was given the responsibility to watch over the entire nation of Israel for his Heavenly Father. His life was not trouble free; it was, however, purposeful and rich. Not many people in the Bible were at the same time a musician, venerable warrior, king, and servant of God like David.

> "Now your kingdom shall not continue. The LORD has sought for Himself a man after His own heart, and the LORD has commanded him to be commander over His people, because you have not kept what the LORD commanded you."
>
> 1 SAMUEL 13:14

DANIEL AND FRIENDS: STRONG CONVICTIONS COME FROM STRONG FOUNDATIONS (DAN. 1)

Daniel (Belteshazzar) and his three friends Hananiah (Shadrach), Mishael (Meshach), and Azariah (Abednego) were taken into captivity from their homeland and deported to Babylon under the rule and command of King Nebuchadnezzar. Brought to serve in the king's court as mere teenagers, the Bible tells us they were bright, healthy, good looking, knowledgeable, and quick learners (Dan. 1:4). But these four friends were also faithful to the Lord. One would think that once teenagers get away from home, they throw off the constraints of their parents and enjoy whatever temptations are available to them. But their parents had instilled in them a powerful sense of what was honoring to God, and they did not depart from it. They distinguished them-selves as having uncommon good sense, morals, and integrity, which were characteristics apparently lacking in their fellow captives taken with them to Babylon. When the king finally had an opportunity to personally examine his court conscripts, he found those who had been faithful to God were head and shoulders above their peers but also above all the existing intelligentsia of his realm. "In all matters of wisdom and understanding about which the king examined them, he found them ten times better than all the magicians and astrologers who were in all his realm" (Dan. 1:20). Every parent hopes their teenagers remember their upbringing and honor their family values when they are away from home. These four friends were a great support to one another and remained faithful even when faced with tremendous adversity (see Dan. 3:17; 6:10).

From Our Family to Yours

[**My mother felt called by God even as a child.**]

My mother tells the story of her brush with death when she was five years old and was rushed to the hospital with a ruptured appendix. Although the doctors fought to save her life, no one thought she would survive. Her mother (Carrie Wells) never left her side, continuing to pray over her even when she slipped into a coma. When my mother finally awakened and began to improve, she remembers her mother's words, "Marilynn, God has saved your life for a purpose. You must always do whatever He wants you to do." That day she committed the rest of her life to God's service and to follow Him regardless of where He led.

Unlocking Your Influence

As you finish looking at truth *consider this...*

1. With which biblical character in this chapter can you identify? How does this story encourage you? What lessons did you learn from it?

GOD AT WORK IN YOUR FAMILY

It may be a stretch for some parents to imagine God using their children significantly in His kingdom work. The messy room, disrespectful remarks, bad attitude, shyness, or social ineptness seem to be insurmountable obstacles. But children grow up and can amaze you with their change in behavior, attitude, and social graces. Never underestimate God, for He has often chosen the insignificant and lowly to accomplish His greatest works. Seeing our children as God does may be one of the greatest challenges we parents face.

Read 1 Corinthians 1:26-29.

> Now remember what you were, my brothers, when God called you. From the human point of view few of you were wise or powerful or of high social standing. God purposely chose what the world considers nonsense in order to shame the wise, and he chose what the world considers weak in order to shame the powerful. He chose what the world looks down on and despises and thinks is nothing, in order to destroy what the world thinks is important. This means that no one can boast in God's presence.
>
> 1 CORINTHIANS 1:26-29, GNB

1. How does this verse relate to your relationship with your children?

One Family's Story

"What better way to teach your children how to minister and love others than to include them in family ministry? Looking back, we see how mission trips have influenced our daughters. For instance, Becca and her twin sisters, Beth and Baileigh, then 3, traveled like champs to Canada for their first mission trip. Along the way, all three made friends with a woman whose husband had been severely injured in an accident. They prayed for both the husband and the woman. They were not told to, they just did.

Mimi is Miriam Holland. She's been called Mimi all her life, even before it became a popular grandmother name!

"Becca had great hopes of going to Boston for its rich history (her favorite subject in school) when the possibility of a trip to Tulsa, Oklahoma, arose. After hearing Mimi's description of the needs for both areas, Becca stood and said, 'Mimi, I really want to go to Boston, but Tulsa needs us more. I vote we go to Tulsa.' Wow, what a proud Mom I was.

"Interestingly, children open doors to homes and families that would normally not be receptive to hearing from strangers. Children don't see color, race, or creed. They just see each other. When children attend our Kid's Club meetings, their parents come to see what is happening. This opens the door to share the gospel with them. It gives the parents an opportunity to share their God stories and Christ with others.

"Family missions give families time together in a very hectic world. It's a time out of the hustle and bustle of everyday life, which is taken for granted by most people. It shows how God's love is for everyone, the weak, the strong, the sick, the elderly, and the lost."—**Sharon and Robbie Moore**

Bringing It Home
→ Ideas your family can use today ←

Child—Help your children choose the story of a character mentioned in the preceding section to act out. Be sure to read the story in the Bible first to make sure you have the details correct. Explain that, just like this character from the Bible, God wants to use them for something significant in the kingdom.

Teen—Most of the people in the Bible faced serious opposition or persecution when they obeyed God. Some were misunderstood, criticized, slandered, or ridiculed publicly. Ask your teen these questions: What do you think is the hardest thing to deal with in obeying God? What would it take to discourage you from obeying God? Is there any one person you would want to stand with you if you were to face opposition? Do you think you would be the one others would choose to stand with them if they were struggling to obey God?

Adult—Sometimes children have a sense of call on their lives. Don't discount what God may be telling your child about being a missionary, doctor, or pastor. Has God been speaking to your children already? Expect that God has called each of your children into His service in one form or another and prepare them now for what they may face in the future.

All Together—Building trust. Have each member of your family stand with their back to the others, cross their arms on their chest, and close their eyes. The rest of the family members gather a few inches behind them with the palms of the hand toward their back. Brace yourself as the person in front slowly falls backward into the hands of their family members. Take turns (even with dad). Be safe; never play with the trust of others. Ask each person how they felt about trusting their family with their life. Ask: "If you can trust your family with your life, can you trust them with secrets? Sharing your dreams or hopes?"

Unlocking Your Influence

As you finish looking at truth, *consider this...*

1. Talk together about your future dreams and plans. Imagine together how God could use you throughout those plans.

2. Discuss a place (city, state, or country) where you would like to do mission work. What draws you to that place? What can you do to make that mission work a reality?

Chapter 6

GOD'S INVITATION
TO YOUR FAMILY

A late night phone call jarred me awake in my hotel room. "We need you to pray!" my wife said. I was out of town and my son Matt was "talking" on the computer with a friend who confided that he was angry, wished his life was over, and suddenly broke off communication. The week before, he had taken a bottle of pills requiring his stomach to be pumped. Matt told my wife, who contacted the friend's mother, and emergency services were dispatched. He was so violent the police needed to restrain him before transporting him to the hospital. At 1:30 a.m. Kim and Matt headed to the hospital to meet the friend. By all accounts my son was incredibly helpful in calming his friend down and convincing him to remain under hospital care. God brought this friend into our lives eight months earlier when he and Matt played on the same basketball team for which I was assistant coach. God had laid this friend on my wife's heart, and our family had been praying for him as he had a troubled past and was currently in foster care. We knew God led us to develop a relationship with him for a reason, but we had no idea just how significant that was going to be. God rarely gives us the big picture until we have been faithful in the small things first. But when we see what God intended to happen down the road, we are so grateful He let us be a part of His plans.

The home you have, the school your children attend, the neighborhood you live in, your job, the person you married, each member of your family, the church you attend, and your activities all provide opportunities for you to be involved with God's work. Because God is all-powerful and all-knowing, He could do everything by Himself. Instead, God chooses to involve His people. In this chapter we will explore some ways God is inviting you to join Him in His plans for the kingdom.

GOD HAS BEEN WORKING IN YOUR FAMILY ALREADY

Not only is your family important to God, but He also desires to use your family significantly in His kingdom work right where you are and in places you have yet to go. The longer you walk with God, the more you come to understand that He truly is in control of your life and circumstances. We may think we have control over our lives and that our plans are working out, but the Bible says differently.

Look at Proverbs 16:9 in several translations:

> "You may make your plans, but God directs your actions."
> GNB

> "A man's heart plans his way, But the LORD directs his steps."
> NKJV

> "In his heart a man plans his course, but the LORD determines his steps."
> NIV

> "A man's mind plans his way, but the Lord directs his steps and makes them sure."
> AMPLIFIED OT

1. In the space provided, write this verse in your own words. Replace the words *you, man,* and *man's* with your family name.

Every aspect of our life and history has God's fingerprints all over it. Whether you know it or not, God has guided you to where you are right now. Yes, we have choices. We can choose to sin and rebel against God and reap the consequences that brings. We are not robots God programmed to fulfill His whims. Rather, as a Christian, His Spirit lives within us and helps us want to do what pleases God, discern God's will, and make choices that align with what God has planned for us. He does this out of His great love for us and out of a deep desire for us to experience Him fully in our lives.

Some people think God first began to work in the apostle Paul's life after his encounter with Christ on the road to Damascus (Acts 22:6). This is not true. God did not first encounter Paul on the Damascus Road. He was there at Saul's birth, as he grew up, and as he went to school. God knew about Paul's academic life and religious zeal, but God had a plan to redirect, use, and turn it into a blessing for others. God used the determination and stubbornness in Paul's youth to keep him standing firm in the midst of terrible persecution and physical abuse later in his life. God even used Paul's Roman citizenship to take the gospel message to the heart of the Roman Empire (Acts 23:11). What Paul counted as worthless (Phil. 3), God used to bring Himself glory. It is a mistake to think that all of your life before becoming a Christian was wasted. God is able to use even our biggest mistakes to bring glory to Himself.

If you think Moses was randomly plucked off the mountainside and enlisted into God's service, consider this: God watched Moses' life from birth and planned to use his training, background, knowledge of the desert, family heritage, and passion to help the Israelites redeem God's people from a life of slavery in Egypt. Even his family lineage and the foster family he grew up in played a significant role in Moses' life and ministry.

2. Think of someone you know whose life before Christ has been used as a powerful testimony to God's work. Write his or her name and a little about how God has used them in the space provided.

From Our Family to Yours

My father and mother came from a long line of committed followers of Christ. Dad's father was a banker and a church planter. Dad was baptized as a teenager by his uncle Lorimar Baker, who served with his aunt Olive as missionaries to

> [God has given
> me a family with
> a rich heritage of
> serving the Lord.
> How about you?
> Take some time to
> thank God for your
> heritage. If you
> can't, that's OK. Ask
> God for that legacy
> to start with you.]

China. His great uncle, Frederick E. Blackaby (1855-1929), went to Spurgeon's College for pastors from 1878-1881 and pastored several churches. Mother's parents served faithfully in their church for decades before going to Zambia, Africa, as missionaries for over five years. Her sister and brother-in-law served many years as missionaries to Eastern Europe before becoming president of a theological seminary in Prague. Her brother and his wife have also faithfully served as pastor and professor in many churches and taught in several theological seminaries. The book *Experiencing God* came not from my father's heart alone; rather, it is the result of generations of faithful service that have impacted his life. Now his five children serve the Lord as pastors, professors, missionaries, and ministers. Several grandchildren are now sensing God's call into full-time Christian ministry.

God has worked through family lines in the past, and He continues to do so today. For those who do not have a family history of faithful followers of Christ, they have the privilege of beginning the heritage for their own family and those who follow after them. We can never overestimate the impact our faithfulness will have upon the generations who follow in our footsteps. "Remember that the LORD your God is the only God and that he is faithful. He will keep his covenant and show his constant love to a thousand generations of those who love him and obey his commands" (Deut. 7:9, GNB).

Knowing and trying to look through God's perspective is crucial. Be on the lookout for God-ordained circumstances, because if you miss them, you have missed a wonderful kingdom opportunity where God wants you to join Him in what He is doing in the lives of those around you.

Read John 12:26.

> "If anyone serves Me, let him follow Me; and where I am, there My servant will be also. If anyone serves Me, him My Father will honor."
>
> JOHN 12:26

3. What does it mean to "follow" Christ? Is this a one-time decision or a lifestyle of daily activity to you?

Look at the following verses and notice the attitude of God's people in several places in the Bible:

> "Mary said, 'Behold the maidservant of the Lord!'"
> LUKE 1:38

> "I commend to you Phoebe our sister, who is a servant of the church in Cenchrea."
> ROMANS 16:1

> "Tychicus, a beloved brother, faithful minister, and fellow servant in the Lord."
> COLOSSIANS 4:7

> "Epaphras, who is one of you, a bondservant of Christ."
> COLOSSIANS 4:12

> "Paul, a bondservant of God and an apostle of Jesus Christ."
> TITUS 1:1

> "James, a bondservant of God and of the Lord Jesus Christ."
> JAMES 1:1

> "Simon Peter, a bondservant and apostle of Jesus Christ."
> 2 PETER 1:1

> "Jude, a bondservant of Jesus Christ, and brother of James."
> JUDE 1:1

God's people are His servants. They need not run around trying to find good things to do for God. Instead, they should wait upon their Master, seeking His heart and finding out what His will is. They should watch to see where God is working around them and join Him in what He has purposed to do through them. Rather than asking God why a situation happened, we need always to ask God what it is He has in mind to do in and through the situation to bring glory to Himself. Ask Him what He has in mind to do through you to make you into a person of spiritual influence. As God's people, we understand that nothing is coincidental for the child of God. God is completely able to work in and through any circumstance at anytime, anywhere, both the good and the bad.

Bringing It Home

[Parents, your young children may not yet understand either the good or bad influence friends have on each other. Use this activity to help them begin to understand.]

Child—Can you name all of your friends? Which ones influence you the most? Which ones do you influence the most? If you asked your friends what they think about you, which of the following words would they use?

○ Bossy   ○ Kind   ○ Selfish
○ Funny   ○ Giving   ○ Loyal
○ Smart   ○ Strong   ○ Athletic
○ Other:_____

Which words would you like them to use about you?

Teen—Think about the friendships you have. Would you categorize them as ones that build you up or tear you down? Are you being a positive or negative influence on others? How? Can you see why God may have brought certain people into your life? How is God using you to impact them for Him?

Adult—Who is the most positive and helpful friend you have? What is it about them that makes you want to be around them? Are you that type of person? If not, why not? Have you asked God to show you how He wants to work through you to influence your friends?

All Together—Ask your family if they want to be the kind of family who influences others and what families they believe God wants you to influence. Avoid making any judgments (such as race, economic situation, needs, difficulties) on why it would not be possible to influence them. Pray that God would bring opportunities in the coming weeks to connect with these families then respond in obedience when He does.

Unlocking Your Influence

As you finish looking at truth *consider this...*

1. Have you begun to recognize how God has directed you down the path of your life and where it has led you? Name some specific times you experienced His direction.

2. Discuss what it means to have the attitude of a servant. Do you have this type of attitude? How can you better have a servant's attitude?

GOD IS IN CONTROL

Take a few moments to consider the details of where God has led you and your family. Think about how God is involved in your life now and even before you acknowledged He existed. Remember, everything God does is entirely intentional. Keep in mind that serving God is not just about being busy as a Christian or doing lots of good works. It is not about us at all but about God and what He wants to accomplish on earth before His Son returns. When you look at the following questions, reflect on what God may be up to in your life and how He may want to work through your family to be a blessing to others. What you see below is meant to open your mind to possibilities of what God may be doing in you and want to do through you.

WHERE YOU LIVE

In 1 Kings 17:7-24 we read about a widow who let Elijah use her spare room when he was near Zarephath. In return, Elijah blessed her home with oil and flour and raised her son from the dead when he grew ill and died. God knew the widow would need Elijah's intervention. It is fortuitous that she was obedient to God and welcomed His servant into her home.

1. Begin to think about how God can use your family right where you live. Check all that apply below.

   ○ We are located in a neighborhood where people can easily gather.
   ○ Our house is big enough to host a small Bible study
   ○ We have extra rooms that we could use for ministry purposes such as hosting traveling missionaries and evangelists, keeping troubled teens, giving temporary shelter to battered women, and so forth?
   ○ Other:_____

Read 1 Kings 17:14. Then take time to pray through the question below.

"The bin of flour shall not be used up, nor shall the jar of oil run dry, until the day the LORD sends rain on the earth."
1 KINGS 17:14

2. Why do you think God led you to this particular house?

YOUR HOME

Your home should reflect God's importance to your family. Rather than your home being a museum of artifacts and precious belongings or a place where people are more important than things, it should be a place where people laugh, hug, and create lasting memories.

Have you dedicated your home to the Lord for His use and purposes? If you are willing, God can use your home as a meeting place for your children's friends where they can feel accepted, welcome, and loved.

1. How can your home become a beacon for the hurting, hopeless, and even other believers in your neighborhood or city? Write your ideas below, and be specific.

[The safe, comfortable environment of your home can be a great tool God can use as you invest in those around you.]

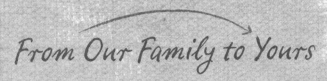

From Our Family to Yours

Our home in Stavanger, Norway, was called the PMC (Pastoral Ministry Center) which housed our family of five, the youth pastor's family, and the church office—all on three levels. We hosted home groups, praise team practices, Bible studies, prayer meetings, church barbecues, and had dozens of kids over for sleepovers! We protected our family life while at the same time offered our house as a blessing to God's people. We have many memories of families who shared a meal with us, who came for birthday parties, or just visited over coffee. These were times that shaped the lives of our children as they grew up and built in them a love for God's people. Now we live in a smaller home. We are no longer able to invite the whole church over, but we share it with smaller groups and individuals as a way to bless others.

KNOWING YOUR NEIGHBORS

What are your neighbor's needs or concerns? You may hold common interests that can either be a bridge to ministering to them or a way you could minister with them to others in your community. Serving the community together can strengthen relationships with fellow believers or begin relationships with non-believers that God could use to draw them to Him.

Everyone comes into contact with others, and God can use even casual relationships to reach those He desires to call as His children. If you neighbor doesn't have a church home, consider inviting their children to go with your family to church or kid's programs. Pray specifically for your neighbors, using their names if possible. Consider asking whether they would be interested in meeting in your home to discuss the Bible even if they attend church elsewhere.

1. Do you know your paper boy, mail carrier, or hairdresser personally? What are some ways can you begin to build a new relationship with someone you don't know well?

2. What do you think God had in mind for you when He placed you in this particular neighborhood?

WHO YOU ARE

Think of special interests each of your family members enjoy, such as music, sports, art, speaking, mime, math, crafts, or other interests. Consider how God could use these things to impact others for His kingdom.

Fill in a chart for each family member, using additional paper if necessary. Gifts would include but are not limited to things such as encouragement, administration, teaching, prayer, and wisdom.

Name _____

Interests _____

Area he/she excels _____

Concerns _____

Friends _____

Calling _____

Gift _____

Name _____

Interests _____

Area he/she excels _____

Concerns _____

Friends _____

Calling _____

Gift _____

Name _____

Interests _____

Area he/she excels _____

Concerns _____

Friends _____

Calling _____

Gift _____

1. Has God placed something or someone on your family members' hearts?

2. Why do you think God placed each member in your family?

3. Do you sense that God has placed a unique calling on any of your children to serve Him? Why or why not? Take some time to write out a prayer for that child in the space below.

[If you have a sense God is calling one of your children, we encourage you to take some time to talk to your pastor about it.]

YOUR WORKPLACE

God wants to use you as salt and light wherever you work, perhaps as you travel to places where missionaries may not be allowed to go, or as you begin a Bible study and pray for others in your workplace. Your family may be able to make friendships with another family or include someone who has no close relatives.

1. How do you think God may want to use you in order to impact others at your workplace?

2. Think about three people at work whom God may want to speak to through you. Write their names here.

Take some time now to begin the habit of praying for these people.

YOUR CIRCLE OF INFLUENCE

Each of us comes into contact with others as we go about our daily lives. You may be surprised at the number of individuals you greet in a week's time. God may have you in organizations, clubs, and teams so your Christian influence can impact others in the group. Parents at your children's school may be willing to pray with you for the children, school, and staff. Family members may join you in regularly praying for relatives who have not made a commitment to Christ.

1. What parents do you regularly see at your children's events? For what reasons may God be bringing them into your path?

2. Take some time today to talk to your spouse about the circles of influence that you are in. How may God want to use you? your spouse? your family? Write your thoughts here.

According to Acts 1:8, we as believers are to be witnesses in the city surrounding us, in our country, and also to the world. Regardless of our job, education, or circumstances, each of us bears this responsibility.

[Pause to think about the impact you can make on the kingdom in the job you're in.]

A Christian piano tuner has the opportunity to go into hundreds of private homes every year and tests them out by playing hymns and Christian songs as he talks to the owners about the Lord. A physician offers to pray with her patients about serious conditions. A home-renovation contractor regularly shares his faith with customers and invites them to his church if they are not attending one. A computer repairman's reputation for fixing computers quickly and treating customers fairly gives him a platform to share his faith. A coach regularly prays with his team before games and encourages a Bible study on character and personal goals. A teacher becomes aware of needs in a particular family and encourages her church to address those needs. A hairdresser regularly engages her clients in conversation and shares with them about her love for the Lord.

THINKING OUTSIDE THE BOX

Do you think you or your family just can't do missions? Let me assure you that many ministries are within your reach. Nearby prisons almost always welcome volunteers. You can pray for prisoners, see if you can volunteer to lead Bible studies, or help care for a prisoner's family.

Local food banks, women's shelters, homeless shelters, and orphanages can use volunteers to provide transportation to church on Sundays or help with Thanksgiving and Christmas meals. Don't forget that many of these organizations operate year-round and can use help on an ongoing basis.

If you're unable financially or physically to travel overseas to minister, you could check on helping at nearby ports or colleges. Folks who are far away from family frequently are open to making new friends. Those relationships can lead to sharing the love of Jesus. That's like foreign missions coming to our backyards!

Resorts, cabins, campsites, apartment complexes, and vacation spots where children or teenagers spend weeks or months at a time are often open to allowing children's clubs, teenage outreach events, day camps, or sports camps. Campsites are also great places to meet when campers might not know where to go for church services. A good Bible-based devotional and some songs sung outdoors are good reminders that we never take a vacation from God.

Both foreign and home missionaries use volunteer help, supplies, prayer, and encouragement. Check with your church or local association office for suggestions. While they appreciate the help, you don't want to overwhelm them. Some are restricted on what they can receive by mail.

Consider speaking with your city mayor or council members regarding how you can pray for them.

1. Where is God working in or near your "box"? How can you and your family join Him in that work?

One Family's Story

"Our Young Married Sunday School class is determined to not just 'learn' the Bible but to 'do' the Bible. Five years ago as we finished the study of *The Purpose Driven Life* we challenged our class to put into practice what we had just learned. One of the purposes we studied was missions. We had been taking an offering regularly for missions, but we felt we were to do more. As young marrieds, we did not have much money, so we determined to combine vacations and mission trips wherever possible. Together we planned several mission trips as families, taking children's mission programs to Native Indians in both Canada and the USA, as well as helping struggling and new start churches. Our first mission trip had 12 adults and 12 children participate. This past year we had 30 children and 25 adults go with us. It is so exciting to see what God can do when families work together."—**Mimi Holland**

No one in God's kingdom is insignificant to God, and He can choose to use anyone He wants to accomplish His purposes. From babies to teens to senior adults, God has done incredible things through every age group.

Unlocking Your Influence

As you finish looking at truth *consider this...*

1. Read the following list of actual missions projects to your family and ask for their responses. This list can open your heart and mind to possibilities of what God can do with families who want to serve Him. Ask your family to pray about opportunities God is preparing now in which your family can join Him.

Softwood Framing Construction Project, Pacific Rim
Backyard Bible Camp Projects, both local and overseas
Log Splitting Evangelism, Serbia
Kidz Games Outreach, Australia
Dixieland Band, Hungary
Community Clean-Up, Bulgaria
Christmas in Serbia—Performing Arts
English clubs, Macedonia
Humanitarian Aid Distribution, Macedonia
Bible Distribution, Turkey
Prayer-walking, Bulgaria
Alpine Prayer-walking, Slovenia
Fishing with Arab Men, Africa/Middle East
Cycling for Souls!, Hungary

Soccer Clinics for Himalayan Villagers, Nepal
Construction, Paraguay
Jesus Film mission trips, France/Spain
Raking leaves for an elderly widow or neighbor
Serving meals at a local homeless shelter
Visiting a nursing home
Give gift baskets to the nurses and doctors at the hospital
Prepare a lunch for the local fire or police department
Help build a home with Habitat for Humanity
Put on a Vacation Bible School at a local apartment or housing complex
Participate in Operation Christmas Child
Help an immigrant family in your community learn English
Buy groceries for a shut-in

GOD IS AT WORK AROUND US

When we come to understand every aspect of our life—including our home, neighborhood, office, hobbies, and vacations—we discover many avenues through which God can impact lives around us, and we begin to see situations and circumstances through His eyes. Every person we sit by, salesman who comes to our door, client we meet, and parent we cheer with at a ball game may, in fact, be God's appointment for us that day.

As Jesus walked in Jericho one day, He met Zaccheus who was sitting up in a tree. Most people would have kept on walking. After all, this man was considered a scoundrel, thief, and traitor. But Jesus saw him as God's appointment for Him that day (Luke 19). Not only was a life transformed for eternity, but a city was impacted by his change of heart. Another day, Jesus happened across a woman drawing water from a well in the afternoon. Most men would not have stopped to talk with her, as she was of questionable character and shunned by the townspeople. But to Christ, she was His appointment for that afternoon (John 4). Not only was her life changed, but a whole town was affected by her transformed heart. One day, Ananias of Damascus was minding his own business when the Spirit of God led him to Judas's house on Straight Street (Acts 9:11). There he met his appointment, Saul of Tarsus, who had been blinded by Christ's glory. Not only was Saul's heart changed that day, but through him, the gospel was taken to much of the known world. As Philip walked along the road, he noticed a foreigner

> " Our whole life will be a series of God-ordained appointments if we have eyes to see what God is up to around us. "

reading the Scriptures. He realized this was God's afternoon appointment for him. He climbed onto the chariot, explained the truths of the Scripture to this government official from Ethiopia, led him to the Lord, and even baptized him! (See Acts 8:26-39.) Our whole life will be a series of God-ordained appointments if we have eyes to see what God is up to around us.

The Bible is full of such appointments where God impacted certain people through His servants. Samuel sought out a young shepherd boy named David who became a king. Paul sought out a young believer named Timothy who became a pastor in a church Paul planted. Jesus sought out twelve men who became His disciples and later His apostles. Paul found a businesswoman named Lydia by a river near Philippi who became the first believer in a newly-established church. Joshua's two spies came across a woman named Rahab in Jericho who became their protector and was later grafted into the people of Israel to become great-great-grandmother to King David. As God's people, our eyes should always be open to the possibility that God is calling on us to be people of influence.

> " Our eyes should always be open to the possibility that God is calling on us to be people of influence. "

[Take the time to prayerfully consider each of these scenarios.]

What might God be up to if …

• your child brings home a friend from school,

• the high school basketball coach requests your help to nurture weaker players on your child's team,

• the parents of a bully at school call to apologize for their child's behavior toward your child,

• you are paired with two coworkers to form a study group to develop project proposals,

• your neighbor asks you to watch her children so she can take her husband to the emergency room,

• you see a man on the street corner with a "will work for food" sign,

• a woman where your child takes swimming lessons is crying,

• a family member is leaving their marriage and has nowhere to go, or

• a church member responds for disaster relief and needs volunteers to go along?

From Our Family to Yours

"We were encouraged to be faithful in little things like helping with a youth mission Bible study, teaching Sunday School, working with kids in vacation Bible school, and let God increase our place of responsibility in His time and in His way. We never sought recognition or influence; we just tried to do well in whatever role God gave us. We learned to be happy with who we are and let God affirm us rather than looking to people for affirmation."—**Mel Blackaby**

[My brother, Mel, recalls how our family served God no matter how big or small our roles were.]

Unlocking Your Influence

As you finish looking at truth *consider this...*

1. Talk together as a family about how you can readily identify God-directed appointments. How can you be alert to God's work in a particular situation? How can you be prepared to join God at a moment's notice?

GOD USES FAMILIES IN PRACTICAL WAYS

Take some time to look over the ideas on the following pages. Check the box beside projects you believe your family could do.

◯ **Send care packages to missionary families or ministry personnel.** These can include toys and collectables missionary kids can't get overseas, certain foods or sauce mixes not locally available, blank Christmas and birthday cards in English, office supplies, family-oriented TV series on DVD, or ask ahead of time for a wish list.

○ **Support missionary projects that need funding to continue.**

Many missionaries are self-funded and much-needed projects are not done due to lack of finances. Digging wells, getting ESL materials and Bibles, renting facilities, purchasing a scooter or motorcycle to take the gospel into remote areas, and other projects can be done if money is available.

○ **Ship Bibles, Bible study material, Christian magazines and resources.**

Many churches in developing and third world countries cannot buy materials to use to disciple and teach new believers. In some cases workbooks are completed in pencil, completely erased, and passed on to the next student. Used Sunday School literature or home group materials are more than many churches in developing countries have currently.

○ **Collect eye glasses.**

Missionaries can use the eye glasses collected through this ministry to open doors to sharing the gospel. Sometimes the missionaries or ministry workers themselves need new glasses but can't afford them! Allowing people to see better can change their lives.

○ **Adopt orphans or help an orphanage.**

Few things have greater immediate impact than taking care of orphans or supporting an orphanage. Adopting an orphan into your family will change the destiny of a child and impact your own family beyond imagination. Collecting clothing, school supplies, medicine, books, or sending money for food, shoes, and necessities is more encouraging than you can imagine. Loving those who have been abandoned is like ministering to Christ Himself. Even going to provide a week of Bible club, crafts, or sports clinics will demonstrate God's love for those who have no one to hug them.

○ **Pray.**

It seems so simple, yet few people realize how important prayer is to missionaries, orphanages, ministries, student outreach groups, churches, mission plants, Bible schools, evangelists, and more. Prayer undergirds all that God's people are doing wherever He has placed them. Many missionaries wait until their birthdays to make important ministry and life decisions because they know people back home are specifically praying for them.

○ **Go on mission trips (city, state, international).**

Praying for others is one thing but actually going yourself is quite another. Many people have never stepped out and gone to provide ministry or service to others. They give, pray, and encourage others but have not experienced the joy of going and serving. Looking into the eyes of grateful people, seeing the joy and excitement children express, and knowing you have made a difference in the lives of others can change your own life radically. Once you've tasted being a part of God's activity, you will not be able to get enough!

⬭ Participate in food drives.

Standing in line to get food for your family can be emotionally difficult, but going and finding out there is not enough food only adds to the pain and disappointment. Most families have more than they need in their homes, and it does not take much effort to organize or participate in a food drive in your neighborhood. Many people are happy to give, and those who receive it will be so grateful they can feed their own children because you cared enough to help out.

⬭ Take music to senior care homes or hospitals.

If you've seen the smiles on the faces and the joy in the eyes of senior adults when children come for a visit to their senior care facilities, you know how easy it is to make a difference in someone's life. Do you play an instrument? Can your family sing a few songs? Do they know how to tell stories? If so, you are ready to bring joy into lives that are often neglected and abandoned by family members, left to spend the rest of their days alone.

⬭ Become pen-pals with missionary kids.

With e-mail, Facebook, MSN, and so forth, it has never been easier to connect with people around the world. But getting an actual handwritten letter still remains an important way to touch the lives of children whose families have moved overseas to do missions work. Getting letters lets them know they are not forgotten and are important, remembered, and prayed for by people in their home country.

⬭ Open your home to Bible studies.

Few things have touched the lives of our children more than regularly having Christians in our home. Our kids always loved the snacks people brought and talking to people who were interested in their lives and happenings. Not only does this help in discipling and encouraging other people as they spend time in God's Word together in your home, but it tells your children that your home is to be shared with others and used to encourage God's people. I am so grateful, even indebted, to our Christian friends who have taken an interest in my children over the years.

⬭ Learn to identify needs.

Ask God to help you be more sensitive to the needs of others. Not everyone can sense what is going on in the lives of others around them. Asking God to help you see through His eyes will create a sensitivity as His Spirit works in you and helps you to see what you can do to encourage others.

⬭ Be aware of resources that can meet needs.

I love to be a resource manager; that is, I keep my ears and eyes open to what people have or can do and help to match their skill or resources with those who have need of them. This helps both the needy and those who love to help others. I know people who keep a "little black book" of Christian friends who are eager to help others using their God-given skills and resources.

○ Honor one another at home to visibly demonstrate Christ's Lordship.

One thing that caught my attention recently is the fact that my children's friends have noticed our family is different than others. We sit down for meals together, are not critical or demeaning of one another, laugh together, and enjoy one another's company. The way we treat one another in our home bears witness to our relationship with God. I believe they notice our love for one another. People notice it, I believe, because it is so rare.

○ Give Christmas presents to others.

Christmas is a great time to work and serve together as a family, putting together shoeboxes to send to needy countries, singing at senior care facilities, writing a family newsletter expressing the reason for the season, sending money typically spent on presents to mission efforts, inviting people into your home for coffee, serving food at shelters, buying presents for needy children, putting together food baskets for low-income families, and so forth. The needs are great, and the opportunities seem endless.

○ Use vacation time/money for mission trips.

If your church does not organize family mission trips, why not begin planning now? For those who cannot afford a vacation and a mission trip, combine them! Helping others is often far more rewarding than you realize. The results of working together as a family and serving the Lord will have both immediate and long-term results in your home.

○ Perform random acts of kindness.

Shovelling snow, chipping ice off sidewalks, putting out salt and gravel, and mowing lawns. The list is endless of what your family can do to bless others.

○ Start up a company.

Many companies have been specifically developed as a tool for God to use in His kingdom. In other words, companies are the instruments or tools to share the gospel, support missions, employ seminary students or part-time pastors, or to demonstrate how God blesses when He is put first in business. The funny thing about these companies is that when they are given over to the Lord for His use and His purposes, He tends to bless them and use them to bring glory to Himself in the community. Does your family have a certain expertise you can use to develop a business God can use to share the gospel or to encourage His people?

○ Engage in medical, agricultural, music, or other specialized missions.

Many churches organize ministries using the skills of their church members. Churches send teams across the globe to help train people in agricultural methods, provide free medical, dental, and eye care clinics to impoverished locations, lead out in sports camps, provide music ministry and even child-care for church or mission conferences where missionaries and ministry personnel meet for their annual conferences.

Build relationships and more through construction projects.

Many families band together and sign up for a variety of construction projects to build a low-cost house, repair damaged churches, renovate missionary housing, construct modest church buildings, build community playgrounds, and so forth, to provide the labor on projects that bring glory to God. It is hard, sometimes very hot and difficult work, but it is a way for your whole family to work together, and it provides the work force to complete desperately needed projects.

Serve through camping ministries.

Many campsites may have a lake, a playground, and a volleyball net but have little, if anything, organized for children. Parents often are delighted to have a safe place that provides crafts, games, snacks, and a Bible story for a few hours each day. Materials from Awana, Vacation Bible School, and kid's Bible clubs can all be modified to teach anywhere from 1-14 days at even remote locations. One parent teaches, the other leads singing, and all the kids help with the games and crafts. Think about safety, plan for hyperactive kids, and watch as God does incredible things to change lives through your efforts.

One Family's Story

"My husband Justin and I believe we have been entrusted with our children to teach them about God and how they can have a living relationship with Him. We have devotions with them every day and love using life's everyday opportunities to teach them about God's order, law, love, and kingdom principles. We share with them about the wonders God does in our family and stand with them as we believe God for big and little things, such as trampolines and puppies. Our biggest prayer is that they would love God with all their hearts all the rest of their lives ... honestly, not that they would be in ministry or be missionaries or pastors as such, but that they would just know God and know how much God loves them. We know if He has access to their hearts, He will lead them in His plan for their lives."—**Gaby Spicer**

WHAT NEXT?

In this book you have seen how God chose specific families from the beginning of time to use for His purposes. Through families, God has blessed and led His people. Through families He has protected and saved His people from enemies. And through families He has provided a model for how His people should relate to one another and function within the church.

So what do you think God has in mind to do through your family? Can you see just how He has put the members of your family in place for a special purpose? The point of this book is not to make your life more complicated or busier but to make the most of your time together as a family and as Christians.

Bringing It Home
→ Ideas your family can use today ←

Child—Ask your child to think about and name three things he can do to help others. Help him think through family members, friends, relatives, and people he doesn't know (such as residents in a senior care facility, people who need food, and so forth).

Teen—Ask your teen, "How do you see God working in your life? Can you think of an example of how you can join in His work at your school or at church?"

Adult—List the five most important things you believe your family learned during this study. What did you do well? What do you want to continue to work on as a family? Compare lists with your spouse.

All Together—Share with each other or act out what you have learned from your other family members.

Unlocking Your Influence

As you finish looking at truth *consider this...*

1. Take a moment to pray, asking God to show you His heart and what He might have in mind for you and your family.

[**Think through what unique gifts your family possesses. What passions has God given each of you?**]

2. Write your family's ministry plan here. Where is God working around your family? How will you join Him in that work?

Immediately: (for example, invite the family next door over for dinner)

In 3 months: (for example, take one day of your family vacation to serve the homeless)

In 6 months:

In 1 year:

All nations will remember the LORD. From every part of the world they will turn to him; all races will worship him. The LORD is king, and he rules the nations. ... Future generations will serve him; they will speak of the Lord to the coming generation. People not yet born will be told: "The LORD saved his people."
PSALM 22:27-28,30-31, GNB

You will be amazed at how many opportunities to be a family of influence are available all around you. May God help your family leave a legacy of faithfulness for generations to follow. We pray that you and your family become a family God Uses!

LEADING A SMALL GROUP

The following ideas will help you prepare for and conduct a seven-session group study of *The Family God Uses*.

SOME THINGS TO THINK ABOUT

What's my role as a group leader?

Don't worry! You do not need to be an expert teacher to lead this Bible study. Your role is more of a facilitator. The group sessions are designed to be interactive and engaging rather than lecture-oriented. In the margin of each group session, you will find suggestions for you to use to keep your group moving and on track.

How often should my group meet?

That's a great question. Most small groups meet weekly. However, with *The Family God Uses* format, your group members may not complete all the content in each chapter in just one week. Here are a few ideas.

Plan ahead. Tell your group members ahead of time what you will be talking about during next week's session so they can be sure to have reviewed those selected sections.

Meet every other week or only once per month. Allow the individuality of your group determine how often you meet together.

Have a retreat. This resource could work great as a seven-session retreat for married couples. You'd simply leave out the Debriefing activities in each session during your retreat. After your retreat, as couples work through chapters 1-6 with their families, encourage them to pair up with other couples from the group to discuss the Debriefing questions together. You might also choose to pair men with men and women with women.

Use in your existing group. If you are already in a group such as a Sunday School class, Bible study, or home-based small group with other couples, you may choose to incorporate *The Family God Uses* into those current meeting sessions. Here's how. Encourage group members to work through one chapter of material per month. Then, once per month forego your existing curriculum and use this small-group guide.

What's the best size for a small group?

The very best small-group dynamics take place in groups of 8-10 members who remain consistent over time (in this case, seven sessions). Smaller groups may be too intimate for some, but if members know and trust one another, smaller groups will be satisfactory too. Larger groups are too big to allow everyone to participate adequately. If you are serious about enabling people to experience all this study has to offer, you don't want to have spectators. If you have more than 15 members, consider dividing into multiple groups.

Family Service Project

One highlight of your small-group experience will be your family service project. In session 2, your group members will begin to plan a service project their families can participate in together. You may choose to lead this effort yourself or to enlist another group member to do so.

PRAY FOR YOUR GROUP

Have you ever shot fireworks on the 4th of July? It's beautiful and a lot of fun—unless they malfunction and do not lift off. If that happens, there's no beauty or fun, just a loud boom. Not bathing your small group in prayer is very similar. God wants to use this study to transform families into lighthouses in their communities. He does the work, not us. Instead of just having a large boom, let's prayerfully seek God and expect Him to do amazing things.

Pray for wisdom. Pray that God will call participants into this study for their benefit and His kingdom work. Pray for marriages and families that are crumbling and that God will bind up the broken pieces. Pray that the families in your group will become families God uses.

HOW TO LEAD A GROUP

1. Remember, as a leader, you can never transform a life. You must lead your group into the power of redemptive community, trusting the Holy Spirit to transform lives along the way.
2. The meeting should feel like a comfortable conversation and not a classroom or lecture experience.
3. Don't talk too much. This will kill a great group experience. A good group leader speaks less than 10 percent of the time.
4. Don't be afraid of silence. If you create an environment where you fill all the gaps of silence, the group will quickly learn they do not need to join the conversation.
5. Every group has individuals who can tend to dominate the conversation. This is unhealthy for the group and frustrating to members. As the leader, try to deal with this assertively yet politely. Say something like, "Thanks,

Kenneth, for your thoughts. Now let's hear from someone we haven't heard from yet."

6. Be sensitive to the Holy Spirit's leading on issues that may need more time. Remember, people and their needs are far more important than completing all the questions.

7. This study does not require a lot of advanced preparation, but do take the time to read through each group session ahead of time. Highlight items you want to be sure to emphasize.

WHAT DO GROUP MEETINGS LOOK LIKE?

Each group meeting consists of four parts:

Connecting
Each group session will begin with fun questions designed to warm the group up and build understanding about other group members. These questions will prepare the group for meaningful discussion throughout the session.

Debriefing
Each group session includes a time to review insights, thoughts, benefits, and ideas you and your family may have gained as you interacted with the study throughout the chapter.

Exploring
This section is the heart of each session. It is an interactive Bible study time designed help members engage God's Word by discussing intriguing and thought-provoking questions.

Transforming
All Bible study should point us to action. That's what this section is all about. Each session ends with a challenge to take the principles you've learned into your families, homes, neighborhoods, and communities and live them out throughout the week. From time to time, you will also discuss practical ideas for mobilizing your group's families to serve together.

Remember, suggestions in the margin will guide you as you navigate your group through each of these sections. Your group will meet for session 1 and begin studying chapter 1 materials for session 2.

Here's an Idea. Capture video footage or still shots of your group during small group sessions and family service project to use during the Commissioning Service at the end of this study.

THE FAMILY GOD USES
SMALL-GROUP COVENANT

It is important that your group covenant together, agreeing to live out important group values. Once these values are agreed upon, your group will be on its way to experiencing Christian community. It's very important that your group discuss these values—preferably as you begin this study. The first session would be most appropriate. (Check the rules to which each member of your group agrees.)

PRIORITY: While you are in this course of study, you give the group meetings priority.

PARTICIPATION: Everyone is encouraged to participate and no one dominates.

RESPECT: Everyone is given the right to his or her own opinion, and all questions are encouraged and respected.

CONFIDENTIALITY: Anything said in the meeting is never repeated outside the meeting.

LIFE CHANGE: We will regularly assess our own life-change goals and encourage one another in our pursuit of becoming more like Christ.

EMPTY CHAIR: The group stays open to reaching new people at every meeting.

CARE AND SUPPORT: Permission is given to call on each other at any time, especially in times of crisis. The group will provide care for every member.

ACCOUNTABILITY: We agree to let the members of the group hold us accountable to the commitments we make in whatever loving ways we decide.

MINISTRY: Members of the group will encourage one another to volunteer and serve in a ministry and to support missions by giving financially and/or personally serving.

I, _____, commit to following the guidelines established for my group. I will strive to glorify God by participating in group discussions and by attending regularly. I will not repeat or discuss anything shared within our group; instead, I will seek to encourage and pray for other group members as we become families God uses.

_____   _____   _____   _____
Signature   Date   Signature   Date

Session 1
INTRODUCTION
SMALL-GROUP EXPERIENCE

CONNECTING (10 MIN.)

[Leader: You may decide that this activity will go longer than 10 minutes to allow group members to get to know one another.]

Begin your group session by learning a little more about each individual participating in the study. If your group is small enough, go around the group and allow everyone the opportunity to answer question 1. Then if time permits, discuss questions 2 and 3. If your group is larger, break into "clusters" of 4-6 people and join back together as a group after this activity.

1. Introduce yourself. Tell about your family and name each family member. What makes each person in your family unique?

2. What are your family's favorite activities? Why do you enjoy doing these things together?

3. Why did you join this study? What do you hope to learn?

DEBRIEFING (15-20 MIN.)

[Leader: Refer to pages 10-11. Take some time to explain how to use the features of this book.]

In the sessions 2-7, this section will guide you in reviewing thoughts, principles, and ideas from the previous chapter studied. This week we will overview *The Family God Uses* Covenant on page 151. Read through it together and sign your name, covenanting to make the most of your group experience.

EXPLORING (15-20 MIN.)

The family God uses is one who seeks after Him and who is prepared to follow Him wherever He desires to lead them. The challenge is to prepare our family in such a way that when God speaks, we are ready to obey. Many children today are facing challenges, temptations, and personal crises but are spiritually unprepared and ill-equipped to handle them.

1. Read Ephesians 6:11-18. What do these verses call us to do to be prepared as Christians in battle?

2. How could putting on the "armor of God" help your family in their daily lives? Be specific and practical.

3. Look again at verse 18. What important action does Paul give at the end of his instructions?

   Unless we as parents get on our knees before the Lord on behalf of our home, children, marriage, and the influence and responsibilities God has given us, we leave ourselves vulnerable to attack, temptation, and being undermined by distractions and challenges. Prayer is going to be the foundation for all that you do and all that you become as a family.

4. What are some things to pray for daily for your family?

TRANSFORMING (10 MIN.)

As you finish your group time today, take some time to pray together.

Pray for ...

• your family as you begin *The Family God Uses* journey together

• fervency in prayer for your spouse and children

• moldable hearts as God reveals His plans for your family

[Leader: Your group may pray together, in clusters, as couples, or one family for another. Decide what works best for your group or do something different each week.]

As you begin working through the content in chapter 1 this week, remember that it is not important to rush through the material to be prepared for your next group session. Rather, the objective is to take adequate time to lead your family to participate in the activities and to understand the ideas presented to you as you begin your journey to becoming a family God uses.

Session 2
GOD'S DESIGN FOR FAMILIES
SMALL-GROUP EXPERIENCE

CONNECTING (10 MIN.)

Again this week, discuss the following questions as a large group or in smaller groups. Start with question 1 and proceed to questions 2-4 as time permits. Enjoy this opportunity to share about the uniqueness of your family.

[Leader: Keep this light-hearted and fun.]

1. What's your favorite television sitcom? How does it portray families? What does that say about the way our culture views family?

2. If someone were to make a movie about your family, would it be a comedy, drama, thriller, or horror flick? Why?

3. What's the best vacation your family has been on together? What made it so special?

4. What do you believe is the biggest threat to today's family?

Families are under attack. The Enemy is strong. The ammunition is live. The threat is real. One of the most important means of protection is building a strong foundation through spending time in God's Word and serving together. Families must take action.

DEBRIEFING (15-20 MIN.)

[Leader: Ask your group to discuss question 1 as couples. After some time, summarize the statements.]

Discuss question 1 with your spouse. After some time, your leader will ask for volunteers who will share thoughts with the whole group.

1. Discuss the Bringing It Home activities you participated in last week. What was the most rewarding part? What was the most difficult? What follow-up conversations do you need to have with your children regarding last week's activities?

2. Read Proverbs 22:6. Then, look back to pages 15-20 and our discussion of God's Purpose for Families. Why do you believe the writer of this proverb didn't use the term *teach, lead, guide,* or something else? What difference does it make?

[Leader: Guide the whole group in a discussion of questions 2-4.]

3. As we discussed the Ten Commandments given in Exodus 20 on pages 21-22, how did you find the commandments relevant to your family? How could obediently following these commandments at all times better help your family? your church? your community?

4. On pages 25-27 we talked about the importance of God's Word to the health of a family. What ideas do you have to give the Word a more prominent place in your home?

[Leader: Guide your group to discuss practical and creative ideas.]

EXPLORING (15-20 MIN.)

As we examine the apostle Paul's ministry, we see families played an important role as he established the very first churches.

1. Read Acts 16:29-34; 18:8; and 1 Corinthians 16:15-18. What is a common thread in each of these Scriptures?

Families were a priority to Paul and central to the churches he started. Most of these churches met initially in the home of one of the families who had come to Christ in that city. Paul stayed long enough in each city where a church was planted to disciple leaders and put spiritual leaders in place to guide the church.

2. What impact would meeting in families' homes have on the church?

3. How do lessons you learn in the home help to prepare you to serve in your local church?

TRANSFORMING (10 MIN.)

Close today's session by thinking about a family service project for your group and family members to complete together sometime between group sessions 6 and 7. Before session 3, pray and ask God to show you where He is currently working and how you and your group can join Him in that work. Come back to session 2 with some ideas to share with the group.

[**Leader:**
Quickly review
the assignments
in chapter 3.
Summarize the next
chapter's ideas and
close in prayer.]

Take some time to pray individually and then pray together.

Pray for ...

• protection for your family in the midst of the Enemy's attacks

• wisdom as you seek to train your children

• ideas for your group's family service project

• other: _____

• other: _____

• other: _____

Session 3
GOD USED FAMILIES TO BUILD THE CHURCH
SMALL-GROUP EXPERIENCE

CONNECTING (10 MIN.)

Think about your immediate and extended family members and your family's heritage as you answer the following questions.

1. Does your family have any traditions? Describe them to the group.

2. Do you have a family heirloom? What makes it special?

3. Were you raised in church? What are your childhood memories or impressions of the church?

Before His birth, during His life, and after His death, many of Jesus' family members impacted God's kingdom. Several other families were influential in the early church. Families have always been instrumental in serving God. Your family can fulfill the purposes He has for your lives today.

DEBRIEFING (15-20 MIN.)

As you studied in chapter 2, the New Testament begins with the story of a young couple, Joseph and Mary, learning they were about to have a son through the miraculous intervention of God's Holy Spirit. The family God chose to use to raise His Son was much like most of ours—hard working, but simple.

[**Leader: Refer to Deut. 6:6-9. Point out that Mary and Joseph evidently were living these principles.**]

1. Recall Joseph and Mary's story on pages 38-39. How do you think Mary and Joseph may have described to their children the ways God intervened in their lives? What difference did it make?

2. What can you learn from Joseph and Mary?

The legacy of your family led many of you to Christ. It may have been the influence of a parent, sibling, aunt, grandfather, or even a cousin that exposed you to the love and hope found in Jesus. God has used families throughout history to build the church and expand His kingdom. Just as the family functions together, so the church functions as a family. Church involvement and fellowship with other believers is a vital part of growing in Christ.

Leader: Ask your group to discuss question 3 as couples. After some time, ask for volunteers to share their thoughts with the whole group.

3. As you reflect on the time you spent together in chapter 2, what was the most meaningful thing your family talked about or participated in?

4. On page 41, Tom and Kim describe the legacy of the Blackaby family. Consider your own family's legacy. What steps can you take to ensure you are leaving a legacy of faith?

5. Based on what you discovered about the significance of families to the early church, how do you think families can play a more active role in spreading the gospel? What could your family do?

6. As you read the section on balancing church and home (beginning on p. 56), did you sense your priorities need to be adjusted? In what way?

EXPLORING (15-20 MIN.)

God never intended His people to be orphans; He provides spiritual families for them to join.

1. Scripture often indicates that the church should be like a family. How do you see that idea reflected in your own church?

2. What makes your church family unique or special? What have you learned in your home that helps you relate to people in your church?

3. Read 1 John 4:9. When you think about what Jesus did for you, what is the first thought that comes to your mind?

In 1 Corinthians 13, Paul gives the benchmark description of what love is. In verse 13 he says, "Now these three remain: faith, hope, and love. But the greatest of these is love" (NIV). Paul wants us to know that the ultimate virtue in which to walk is love. Love is the highest value of our lives.

Leader: Be sure to leave time to emphasize a discussion of questions 4-5.

4. Now read 1 John 4:11. What barriers have kept you from demonstrating God's love to others?

5. If you listed the top three values of your family, what would they be?

1.

2.

3.

TRANSFORMING (10 MIN.)

Make a list on a dry-erase board of the family service project ideas God brought to your attention this week. Discuss which ideas would be the best suited for your group members and their families, recognizing what each person can contribute to the project. Narrow the list to a few ideas, and pray for God to reveal what He is calling your group to do for Him.

As you finish your group time today, take some time to pray together. Be creative. You may choose to have spouses or couples partner together. Another option would be to divide the group into three clusters and ask each cluster to pray for each of the different needs listed below.

Pray for ...

• your relationships with other believers and unbelievers

• you to love others as God does

• God to align all group members' hearts for your family service project

[**Leader: Quickly review the assignments in chapter 4. Summarize the Transforming section in your own words and close in prayer.**]

THE CHURCH AS GOD'S FAMILY

SMALL-GROUP EXPERIENCE

CONNECTING (10 MIN.)

Think about each individual in your family as you answer the following questions. Have fun and feel free to be creative with your responses.

[Leader: Share your responses to one of these questions to get the group started.]

1. What does your family enjoy doing together? Be specific.

2. Imagine each person in your family is an animal. What animal would they be? Why?

Just as we have unique family members in our homes, we also have unique family members in our churches. In chapter 3, you studied how God designed the church to function like the family, as brothers and sisters serving and loving through Christ.

DEBRIEFING (15-20 MIN.)

[Leader: Guide your group's discussion of questions 1-4.]

1. On pages 69-70, we talked about sharing the good news of Jesus. With whom do you find it most difficult to share the gospel? Is it a friend, coworker, family member, or someone else?

2. Look back to your list on page 76. What things do you have listed under "church"? Under "home"? Compare your list with others'. What can you learn from someone else's list?

[Leader: You may choose to ask a group member to read Milne's story aloud.]

3. Read Bruce Milne's thoughts in One Family's Story on pages 78-79. How does his dream differ from reality within your sphere of influence?

4. Discuss with your group your answer to question 1 on page 81.

EXPLORING (15-20 MIN.)

"We will serve the Lord" was not just a nice catch phrase for the Israelites in Joshua 24. It was a commitment they had made. But even though God's people said they were committed to following God (Josh. 24:16-17), they had not cleared out the idols back in their homes.

[Leader: Read Josh. 24:16-17,23 aloud.]

1. Are there things in your home or things that you do or say that could become a stumbling block to your children? What steps can you take to remove these stumbling blocks?

2. What does "incline your heart to the Lord" mean? What types of things would prevent you from doing that?

3. What is it about your life that your children could point to that indicates you are seeking after God?

4. What challenges in your family do you feel will be difficult to overcome?

5. What does Jeremiah 32:27 say about challenges your family may face?

[Leader: Allow married couples to discuss question 1 together. Ask for volunteers to share their responses, then direct group discussion of questions 2-5 as time allows.]

TRANSFORMING (10 MIN.)

Decide as a group what your family service project will be. Plan to complete it between sessions 6 and 7. Make a to-do list of all preparation tasks and assign duties to individuals. Continue to pray for the ways God will use your group members and families in His work.

As you finish your group time today, take some time to pray for ...

• courage for you and your family members to share the good news of Jesus with others

• the ability to overcome challenges and stumbling blocks your family may face

• details of your family service project to come together

Session 5
BECOMING A FAMILY GOD USES
SMALL-GROUP EXPERIENCE

CONNECTING (10 MIN.)

[Leader: If your group is small enough, allow time for everyone to share. If not, you may choose to divide them into clusters of 4-5.]

The following questions may involve some very personal information. Do not feel obligated to share any details that may make you feel uneasy. Only share information that you feel is comfortable and appropriate.

1. Briefly tell the story of your spiritual journey. Include your personal encounter with Christ and church experience.

2. What is one of the most meaningful things your parents taught you? Why?

We have all been influenced throughout our lives by our earthly parents. As Christians, our lives have also been impacted by our Heavenly Father. He must be our central focus if we intend to become a family He uses.

DEBRIEFING (15-20 MIN.)

1. On page 84, you were asked which other gods fight for your devotion and attention. What distracts you from God? How might this distraction give your children an improper representation of your devotion to God?

[Leader: Compile a list of the verses group members suggest while answering question 2 and e-mail the list to the group.]

2. Kim recommends Scripture memorization on page 91. What verses give you strength and encouragement in difficult situations?

3. Discuss the areas of your life in which you find it most easy and most difficult to trust God. What things are your children learning from your dependence on God?

4. How does having an eternal focus impact your family? your daily routine? your priorities?

5. Share your family's spiritual markers that came to mind as you read pages 103-105.

EXPLORING (15-20 MIN.)

1. Ask a member of the group to read aloud Luke 18:17.

   Jesus says entrance into His kingdom requires us to be like children. This action is "child-like" not "childish"! It is also sometimes hard for adults to grasp. Put yourself in the place of one of your children or grandchildren to answer question 2.

2. Who do children depend on the most? Who do they rely on for protection? comfort? Who do they love more than anyone else in the world?

   It is that dependence, simple faith and trust, and undying devotion that God is looking for in the heart of each person who enters His kingdom. God is not our colleague, peer, assistant, or servant; He is our Father.

3. Identify the areas, if any, in your life where you have "outgrown" your need for God.

4. Read Ephesians 6:4 in your Bible.

5. Did God show you some things as a child that you still recall? What are they? Note ways you can share these truths from God with your children.

[Leader: Guide your group to discuss practical and creative ideas.]

TRANSFORMING (10 MIN.)

Be sure that everyone has completed their assigned preparation tasks from session 4 for your family service project. If additional tasks have come up or other resources need to be gathered, divide up duties among group members. Finalize the date and time, and pray for God to prepare you for His work.

As you finish your group time today, take some time to pray for ...

• your children to have a craving for God

• prepared hearts for your group members and families as you serve through your family service project

Session 6
GOD USES CHILDREN
SMALL-GROUP EXPERIENCE

CONNECTING (10 MIN.)

As you answer these questions, try and put yourself in the place of your children. Try to imagine why they think and act in the ways they do.

[Leader: Invite group members to show pictures of their children as they answer questions 1-2.]

1. Describe something funny one of your children has said or done. Why is it so funny to you?

2. What is your children's favorite bedtime story? Why?

Children possess a simplicity in life that most adults cannot fully grasp. But, as you've read through chapter 5, you saw that God is clearly working in and through the lives of children.

DEBRIEFING (15-20 MIN.)

[Leader: Ask a group member to read Mark 10:13-16 aloud as you answer question 1.]

1. Look back at your answers on page 108. What do you think hinders adults from coming to Christ like a child as commanded in Mark 10:13-16? On pages 108-109, Tom and Kim describe some characteristics of children. Which ones do you believe are most important for adults to live out?

2. On page 111, you answered a question about your most vivid childhood memories. Discuss them and how they've changed in your adult life.

3. Recall Tom and Kim's description of children God uses on pages 115-116. Of the children used in the Bible described on pages 116-120, which one stood out to you? Why?

4. What did you learn about your individual family members through the trust-building activity in "Bringing It Home" on page 123? Did it reveal some areas of strength you can continue to build on or areas of weakness you need to work on? Discuss your family's reactions.

EXPLORING (15-20 MIN.)

God calls every family to serve Him. He is at work around us even now. The real question is whether or not we are ready, willing, and have our eyes open to the opportunities He places before us every day.

1. Read the following verses: Colossians 4:7,12; Titus 1:1; James 1:1; 2 Peter 1:1; Jude 1:1. What word do they have in common?

2. Does your family reflect the heart of each person you just read about?

3. In what ways does your family seek the Master to hear what He has for His servants to do each day?

4. What opportunities to serve the Lord have you come up for your family in the past two weeks?

5. How did you recognize these opportunities as God's invitations to be a part of His activity?

[Leader: Instruct members to take a few minutes to answer question 1 on their own. You may play some light music to set the mood. After a few minutes, call the group back together and proceed with question 2.]

TRANSFORMING (10 MIN.)

Discuss your final plans for your family service project. Remind everyone of the date and time. Delegate any remaining tasks or responsibilities. Be sure that you have someone assigned to take pictures and capture video footage to use in the Commissioning Service. Take some time to bathe your project in prayer.

Pray for:

• God to use your efforts for His glory

• your children to have an experience that will be the first of many godly encounters in their lifetime

• what God might teach your family through participating in this service project

[Leader: If any group members have missed session 6, call and remind them about the family service project.]

GOD'S INVITATION TO YOUR FAMILY
SMALL-GROUP EXPERIENCE

CONNECTING (10 MIN.)

1. Describe your neighborhood to the group. What could you do to get to know those families better?

2. Share about a time when you have sensed God working around you and you joined Him in that work. How did that experience make you feel? What did you learn from it?

God has been and will continue to work through your family if you are obedient to Him. As you complete this study, prayerfully consider how you can greater impact those around you and around the world for His kingdom.

DEBRIEFING (15-20 MIN.)

[Leader: Share the pictures and video footage from your family service project with the group.]

1. Talk about your family service project. What did God show you? What did your family enjoy most about the project? least?

2. What has been the most beneficial part of this study to you? your family?

3. Regardless of where, when, and how an individual comes to know Christ, God uses each person in His kingdom. How do you see God specifically using your family in His work?

4. Of the areas outlined on pages 131-137, in which is your family most impacting others? What makes this your family's strength? How might you use these characteristics to further your family's influence in other areas?

5. Practical ways your family can serve together are listed on pages 141-145. What can you do to ensure that your family follows God's leading to minister to others?

EXPLORING (15-20 MIN.)

We've seen throughout the pages of this study that God has used families since the beginning of time. God used families to bless others in the Old Testament, He used families to establish churches in the New Testament, and He uses families today to share the truth of His love to others around them.

1. Do you feel your family is ready to be a family God uses? Why or why not?

2. Is there anything preventing you from letting God use your family?

[Leader: Guide your group members to pair up with their spouses to answer question 2. After some time, call the group back together.]

Read Deuteronomy 6:5.

> "You shall love the LORD Your God with all your heart, with all your soul, and with all your strength."

3. Loving God with all of your heart, soul, and strength implies action on our part. How will your family demonstrate your love for God this week? this month? this year?

4. Take a moment to list five people or families God has brought across your path that you believe He wants to impact through your family:

1.

2.

3.

4.

5.

TRANSFORMING (10 MIN.)

As you wrap up this session, look back at your family's ministry plan on page 147. Discuss as a group how you can keep each other accountable to what you believe God is leading you to do. Spend some time in prayer. Match couples together to pray for one another or pray as a whole group, each person praying aloud for another group member. Pray specifically for the person and the family's influence as God uses them in their neighborhoods, communities, schools, and around the world.

[Leader: Be sure that someone prays for each group member specifically.]

GROUP MEMBER DIRECTORY

Name:_____ Phone number_____
E-mail address_____

Name:_____ Phone number_____
E-mail address_____

Name:_____ Phone number_____
E-mail address_____

Name:_____ Phone number_____
E-mail address_____

Name:_____ Phone number_____
E-mail address_____

Name:_____ Phone number_____
E-mail address_____

Name:_____ Phone number_____
E-mail address_____

Name:_____ Phone number_____
E-mail address_____

Name:_____ Phone number_____
E-mail address_____

Name:_____ Phone number_____
E-mail address_____

Name:_____ Phone number_____
E-mail address_____

Name:_____ Phone number_____
E-mail address_____

Name:_____ Phone number_____
E-mail address_____

Name:_____ Phone number_____
E-mail address_____

FAMILY GOD USES CHALLENGE

Today our family accepts God's call to be a family God uses in our home, in our community, and wherever He may lead us. We accept the responsibility of being a family of influence in our place of work, our schools, and in every area of our life. We are determined together to leave a legacy of faithfulness for generations to come.

"As for me and my house, we will serve the Lord."
JOSHUA 24:15

Family members:

Signed_____ Date_____

Signed_____ Date_____

Signed_____ Date_____

Signed_____ Date_____

Signed_____ Date_____

Signed_____ Date_____

Signed_____ Date_____

Group leader/pastor

Signed_____ Date_____

Begin to list ways God uses your family in the days, months, and years to come:

1.

2.

3.

4.

A FAMILY COMMISSIONING SERVICE

Use this outline to commission families in your church who have completed *The Family God Uses*. Prior to the service give each worshiper a copy of the responsive reading as accompanist plays "People Need the Lord."

WELCOME TO WORSHIP (PASTOR)

Pastor begins the service, welcoming the congregation in his own unique way and briefly describing *The Family God Uses* study (the group leader may participate in this portion of the service). Say something like, "It has been said that families that pray together, stay together. That's a great thought. We believe, though, that families who *serve* together stay together. Over the past seven weeks, ____ of our families have been involved in a Bible study called *The Family God Uses*. They have worked through seven sessions learning how to get and keep their family God-centered as they teach their children their role in God's kingdom. These families are committing to pray, grow, and serve together. They are looking to discover where God is at work around them and to learn how to join Him in that work. So today, we're here to commission them to be missionaries in the neighborhoods, PTA's, sports teams, book clubs, and homes in which God has placed them."

WORSHIPING TOGETHER (WORSHIP LEADER)

Song suggestions include "A Christian Home"[1] and "In Christ Alone."[2] For other song choices visit www.*lifewayworship.com*.

CALL TO SERVICE (PASTOR/FAMILIES)

Pastor reads Isaiah 6:1-8, then says something like, "Here we see that when the prophet Isaiah encountered the very presence of God, he was humbled and said, "I am a man of unclean lips." In verse 8, Isaiah, from his humility, answered God's call to serve Him in whatever capacity He may require. Isaiah said, "Here am I. Send me!" Tonight we have ____ families who are saying to God the very same thing Isaiah did." Introduce those families to the congregation. You may choose to put their pictures on your screen as you introduce them.

TESTIMONY (FAMILIES)

Enlist one or two families to share how they have recognized God at work around them and are ready to join Him in it. Or if you made your own video during the group sessions or the group mission project, you may use it. Other video ideas can be found at *www.sermonspice.com*.

PRESENTATION (PASTOR)

Give each family a certificate (available for print at *www.lifeway.com/e2/shop/?R=834384*) signed by the pastor and staff and a family devotional book such as *Experiencing God Day by Day*.

AFFIRMATION (CONGREGATION)

Pastor has families being commissioned come forward and leads the following reading.

Congregation: Our church believes that all people have been called by God into His service to use their spiritual gifts and talents in kingdom work.

Worship Leader: We also believe that God strategically places each person and each family so that He can use them in unique and significant ways to impact the lives of people around them.

Families being Commissioned: We believe God has called us to serve our community and are answering His call. Here we are, Lord. Send us!

Congregation: We also believe that these families cannot accomplish God-sized tasks on their own and need the full support, encouragement, and equipping of a whole church family.

Worship Leader: Today we want to pray for these families, asking God to guide them, protect them, and help them to do what He asks them to do so that together we can rejoice in what God accomplishes through them to change lives for eternity.

PRAYER (CONGREGATION)

Have the congregation gather around the families, lay hands on them, and pray for them.

SPECIAL MUSIC

Some song ideas include "Do They See Jesus In Me" by Joy Williams[3] and "Find Us Faithful" and "The Mission" by Steve Green.[4]

CLOSING PRAYER (PASTOR OR GROUP LEADER)

"Father, you created these families and placed each member in them on purpose. You knew the victories, challenges, and successes they would have as they established their homes and grew in their love and support for one another. They have committed their lives to You and asked You to be a part of their homes. They have given their homes to You for Your use and now commit to Your service. We don't know the challenges they will face, but You do. You brought them to be a part of our church family, so we commit this day to pray for them, support them, encourage them, and help them however we can as they represent our church family in the community and serve You in Your kingdom work. May they each come to know You more personally and may their love for You deepen as they work together to seek and serve You. May you receive all the glory. In the name of Jesus Christ we pray. Amen."

1. "A Christian Home," No. 54, The Baptist Hymnal, 2008.

2. "In Christ Alone," No. 506, The Baptist Hymnal, 2008.

3. Lyrics may be accessed at www.music-lyrics-gospel.com.

4. Lyrics may be accessed at www.stevegreenministries.org.

ADDITIONAL RESOURCES

BOOKS

The Family God Uses: Leaving a Legacy of Influence by Tom and Kim Blackaby (Birmingham, AL: New Hope Publishers, 2009).

Anointed to be God's Servants: How God Blesses Those Who Serve Together by Henry and Tom Blackaby (Nashville, TN: Thomas Nelson Publishers, 2005).

Family Worship: in the Bible, in History, & in Your Home by Don Whitney (Shepherdsville, KY: The Center for Biblical Spirituality, 2006).

Parenting Prodigals: Six Principles for Bringing Your Son or Daughter Back to God by Phil Waldrep (Friendswood, TX: Baxter Press, 2001).

The Power of a Praying Parent by Stormie Omartian (Eugene, OR: Harvest House Publishers, 1995).

The Power of a Praying Husband by Stormie Omartian (Eugene, OR: Harvest House Publishers, 2001).

Experiencing God: Knowing and Doing the Will of God by Henry Blackaby and Claude King (Nashville, TN: LifeWay Press, 2007).

A God Centered Church: Experiencing God Together by Henry and Melvin Blackaby (Nashville, TN: B&H Publishing Group, 2007).

Dynamic Diversity: Bridging Class, Age, Race and Gender in the Church by Bruce Milne (Downers Grove, IL.: IVP Academic, 2007).

Building Faith at Home: Why Faith at Home Must be Your Church's #1 Priority by Mark A. Holmen. (Ventura, CA: Regal Books, 2007).

Unlimiting God: Increasing Your Capacity to Experience the Divine by Richard Blackaby (Colorado Springs, CO: Multnomah Books, 2008).

Parents' Guide to the Spiritual Growth of Children by John Trent, Rick Osborne, Kurt Bruner (Colorado Springs, CO: Tyndale House Publishers, 2000).

801 Questions Kids Ask About God: With Answers from the Bible by Rick Osborne (Carol Stream, IL: Tyndale House Publishers, 2000).

The Singing Bible: The Fun & Easy Way to Learn Scripture (Compact Disc) by Focus on the Family (Carol Stream, IL: Tyndale House Publishers, 2007).

OTHER RESOURCES

Parenting resources by Rick Osborne available at *www.ChristianParentingDaily.com* and *www.rick-osborne.com*.

Focus on the Family
Mission Statement: "To cooperate with the Holy Spirit in sharing the Gospel of Jesus Christ with as many people as possible by nurturing and defending the God-ordained institution of the family and promoting biblical truths worldwide." Focus on the Family has a tremendous track record for helping families and providing good resources for parents and children to strengthen them in the Lord and to help them face the challenges of life. *www.focusonthefamily.com*.

PRAYER RESOURCES

Pray Magazine—*www.praymag.com*
PrayKids!—*www.praykids.com*
IMB Kids On Mission Pray—*http://kompray.imb.org*

ORGANIZATIONS & MINISTRIES WHERE FAMILIES CAN SERVE OR FIND MISSION OPPORTUNITIES

Union Gospel Mission—Located in several cities throughout North America
The Salvation Army—*www.salvationarmy.org*
North American Mission Board—*www.namb.net*
International Mission Board—*www.imb.org*
Operation Mobilization—*www.om.org*
ShortTermMissions.com—*www.shorttermmissions.com*
Adventures in Missions—*www.adventures.org*
SEND International—*www.send.org*